Automotive Electronics

Servicing Guide

By

Joseph J. Carr

HOWARD W. SAMS & CO., INC.
THE BOBBS-MERRILL CO., INC.
INDIANAPOLIS · KANSAS CITY · NEW YORK

FIRST EDITION

FIRST PRINTING—1973

Copyright © 1973 by Howard W. Sams & Co., Inc., Indianapolis, Indiana 46268. Printed in the United States of America.

All rights reserved. Reproduction or use, without express permission, of editorial or pictorial content, in any manner, is prohibited. No patent liability is assumed with respect to the use of the information contained herein.

International Standard Book Number: 0-672-20927-6
Library of Congress Catalog Card Number: 72-84435

Preface

In the past few years the automotive electronics field has grown in tremendous proportions. A decade ago the only automotive entertainment electronics available was the standard pushbutton a-m radio. In comparison, today we have an assortment of tape players, as well as a-m, am/fm, and am/fm/fm stereo (some with built-in tape player) radio combinations. With this influx of electronic equipment to the automotive field, the technician might find himself in a dilemma. The days of the screwdriver mechanic are long gone. The auto radio technician of today should be as proficient at electronic troubleshooting as a color-tv technician.

It is the purpose of this book to present the knowledge that an individual needs to be proficient in automotive electronic servicing. Starting with a basic review of superheterodyne theory, you are taken step by step through circuits, stages, and sections of complete tape players (both cassette and eight-track), as well as fm, fm stereo, and a-m radio. Current is traced through the complex circuitry to assure the reader's complete understanding of the subject.

Integrated circuits (ICs) have made their way into car radios. With various car radio circuits being delegated to the integrated circuit or *chip,* a working knowledge of ICs is required to service a car radio. As well as ICs, signal-seeker radios have been included to further advance the reader's knowledge of automotive electronics.

Since the radio of today is of much better quality and extremely more complex than its predecessors, the need for qualified technicians to service such units is expanding every day. The demand may be met by many technicians, but only the *qualified* technicians will have the knowledge to do the job properly. This book will provide that knowledge.

JOSEPH J. CARR

Contents

Chapter 1

A-M Car Radio Circuits

The standard a-m radio is the basic style of automobile receiver. The vast majority of car radios sold every year are a-m only units. Even most of the fm sets are, in reality, am/fm radios.

REVIEW OF BASIC
SUPERHETERODYNE THEORY

Early radios were difficult to adjust and were somewhat less than efficient. These radios used several rf amplifier stages (tuned to the frequency of the station being received) and a regenerative detector. However, many problems arose from this system since it is almost impossible to make all of the rf amplifiers *track* the same frequency at the same time. Also, as the frequency of operation went higher, the effectiveness of the rf amplifiers was reduced, and the adjustment of the regenerative detector became more critical. Radios of this design were called *tuned radio frequency* (trf) receivers. The modern *superheterodyne* radio was invented to overcome the faults considered inherent in the trf type of radio.

Simply stated, heterodyning is a process of mixing together two frequencies to produce a third frequency. An example of heterodyning can be produced on almost any musical instrument. Go to a piano, strike a key (middle C) and note the tone. Next, strike the key above middle C. The next higher key is D. After noting the new tone and its difference from the first, strike both keys at the same time. The tone heard now is a mixture of C and D. When two tones are mixed together under the right conditions, they generate at least two new tones, in this case, C + D and D − C. This applies equally well to radio signals. In a superheterodyne radio, the signal picked out of the air by the antenna and amplified by an rf amplifier is mixed with a locally generated signal to produce a third frequency that is lower than either of the other two (the difference signal). In car radios, the usual practice of American designers is to use a variable-frequency oscillator (vfo) operating 262.5 kHz above the frequency being received as the source for the local mixing signal. When heterodyned with the rf amplifier signal, this will produce a difference signal of 262.5 kHz.

The purpose of the superheterodyne receiver (the "super" prefix is from advertisers, while the original term was "heterodyne" radio) is to convert the rf signal to a lower frequency so that maximum gain, effectiveness, and stability can be realized. It is almost always easier to achieve high gain with good stability at a single, lower frequency. A single-frequency stage is much easier to neutralize than a variable-frequency stage. Also to be considered is that the effectiveness of most tuned circuits decreases at higher frequencies. Because of this, the superheterodyne offers superior performance on opposite ends of the same bands or on different bands when compared to the trf type of radio. Can you imagine trying to negotiate interstate or downtown traffic while trying to constantly fiddle with a trf-regenerative detector radio? After the signal is processed by the rf amplifier, the frequency converter, and an i-f (intermediate frequency) amplifier, it is fed to a detector where the audio portion of the program is removed. This audio signal is then fed to tone shaping circuits, then to an audio amplifier system, and finally to the speaker.

STAGES IN A SUPERHETERODYNE RECEIVER

There are several different stages in a superheterodyne (superhet) receiver. However, they are all interrelated to each other. This fact should be kept in mind as you proceed through the text.

RF Amplifier

The radio frequency (rf) amplifier, which is the first stage in the radio, is fed by the antenna. Since signals from the antenna are extremely weak, the rf amplifier must strengthen the signal of interest and attenuate all others. In all modern car radios, a transistor provides the amplification, while tank circuits consisting of inductors and capacitors provide the attenuation.

Converter

The purpose of this stage is to convert the rf signal to a lower frequency by means of heterodyning. There are two basic types of converters, only one of which is properly called a converter. One system, used in only a few a-m car radios, uses separate vfo and mixer transistors. The true converter, however, found almost universally in a-m car radios, uses a single transistor to provide both mixer and local oscillator functions.

I-F Amplifier

The i-f amplifier provides the bulk of amplification required to bring the signal up to an amplitude sufficient to drive the detector stage. The i-f amplifier must also provide most of the discrimination against unwanted signals (selectivity). In almost all American car radios, 262.5 kHz has been chosen as the i-f. In most American home radios and in European car radios, the i-f is either 455 kHz or 460 kHz. In American car radios, however, it is rare to find such an i-f.

Detector

The purpose of the detector is to extract the program audio that has been modulated on the carrier.

Audio Amplifier

The audio stages amplify the weak voltage delivered by the detector, shape its tonal characteristics, and pass it on to the power amplifier. The power amplifier is a special type of audio amplifier that increases the power level of the signal. The other types of audio stages (preamplifiers and driver amplifiers) simply increase the voltage amplitude of the signal. The output from the power amplifier is used to drive the speaker system.

Speaker

The speaker is an electromechanical transducer that converts the electrical signal energy delivered by the power amplifier to a mechanical (or acoustical) vibration which the ear can detect.

Automatic Gain Control (AGC)

Agc, also called automatic volume control (avc) is used to reduce loudness differences as you tune across the various stations on a dial. A well-designed radio can respond to weak signals as well as strong signals. If your radio did not have agc and the volume control was turned up loud enough to hear the weak stations, you would be blasted out of the car when you suddenly tuned to a really strong local station. To help limit that blasting and to save the eardrums, modern radios use an agc circuit that lowers the overall gain of the radio on strong stations and increases the gain for weak stations.

STAGE DESIGNS

Fig. 1-1 shows the typical superheterodyne found in all but a few automobile radio designs. It can be used as a reference point as the designs of each stage are discussed. This book will not concern all

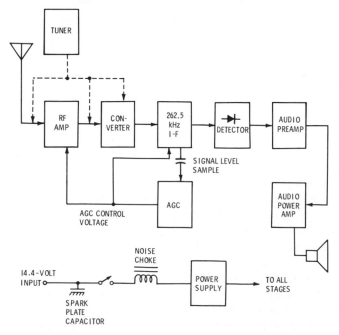

Fig. 1-1. Block diagram of a superheterodyne radio.

types of car radio circuits, but rather those that can be considered either typical of a large number of existing radios or sufficiently unique to warrant consideration.

RF Amplifier

The circuit shown in Fig. 1-2 is typical of many solid-state rf amplifier designs in car radios. This circuit and close variations have been in use for over 10 years. This particular stage is from a Delco car radio designed and produced by the Delco Electronics Division of General Motors. Notice that variable tuning is accomplished by adjusting the powdered-iron slugs of the tuning coils, rather than by the use of variable capacitors. The variable capacitors shown in Fig. 1-2 are used to trim the coils so that they will all track on the same frequency. This is standard procedure on car radios. Home radios normally use two or three variable capacitors coupled together (ganged) as the main tuning control. In those sets, you must trim the coil and sometimes a very low-value trimmer capacitor to obtain proper tracking. Car radios, however, have followed a different procedure because of the design requirements of pushbutton tuners. The mechanical assembly which gangs together all of the coil slugs is called a *permeability tuning mechanism* (PTM). The PTM is driven by a linkage system connected to either a manual or a pushbutton tuning assembly.

Resistor R1 serves to stabilize the emitter circuit of the rf amplifier stage. Bias to this type of

stage is supplied by the agc voltage connected to the base terminal of transistor Q1 via resistor R2 and the secondary winding of coil L2. The dc return is through coil L3 and resistor R3, connected between ground and the collector terminal of transistor Q1.

Fig. 1-3 shows a simplified schematic of the rf amplifier stage. For clarity, all the circuitry, except for that in the dc path, has been removed. The total current drawn by the stage flows down through resistor R1. Inside the transistor, two currents combine to create this total current. The majority of the current, in excess of 95%, flows down from the collector circuit. The remaining current flows into the base from the agc line. From a servicing technician's point of view, there are three significant voltages in this type of circuit. One is the base-to-emitter bias voltage. In radios using germanium transistors, this will run close to .2 volt, while in radios with silicon transistors, the value will be closer to .6 volt. The last two significant voltages offer a good indication of how much current the stage is drawing—the voltage drop across the emitter resistor and the collector-to-ground voltage. The bias voltage and the two conduction voltages will vary directly with the agc control voltage. The agc control voltage is proportional to the strength of the received signal.

Fig. 1-4 shows an rf stage using an npn transistor. Rf signals are decoupled or bypassed to common ground by capacitor C1. The function of this capacitor is to place the lower end of the input coil secondary at ac ground potential while keeping it above ground as far as the dc bias voltage is concerned. It does this because a capacitor will pass ac while at the same time it blocks dc. Notice that in this type of stage the emitter is connected close

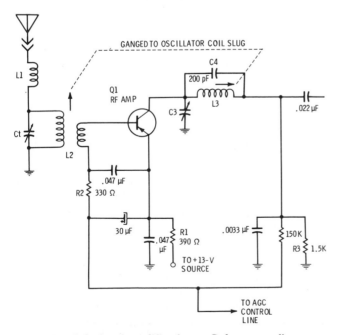

Fig. 1-2. An rf amplifier from a Delco a-m radio.

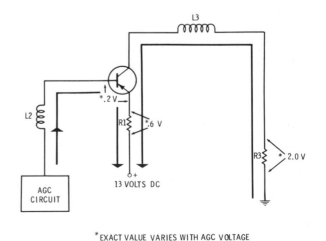

Fig. 1-3. Current in a simplified rf amplifier.

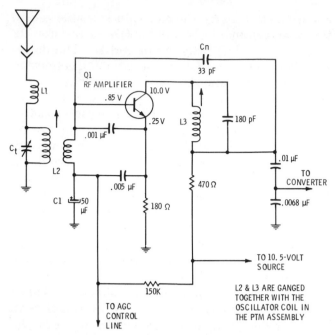

Fig. 1-4. An rf amplifier from a Bendix a-m radio.

to dc ground (negative side of the battery on most American automobiles), while the collector is tied to the positive side of the battery. In the pnp stage of Fig. 1-2, the opposite is true. This is due to the polarity differences of the respective types of transistor. Other than that, the two stages are essentially the same.

There are two facets to the ac signal path in the rf amplifier stage. One is the bypassing or decoupling ac path, while the other is the frequency-selective (tuning circuits) signal path. Fig. 1-5 illustrates two examples of tuned circuits.

Although the preceding rf amplifiers show only two apparent tuned circuits, there are in reality three. In Fig. 1-2, the primary of coil L2 is tuned to the frequency of the station being received. The capacitor, C_t, is called the antenna trimmer capacitor. Besides tuning the coil, it also acts to compensate for differences in antenna cable capacitance. It is usually adjusted when the radio is originally

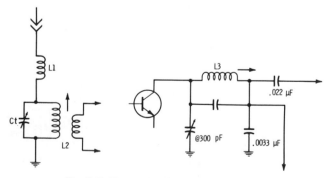

Fig. 1-5. Two examples of tuned circuits.

installed in a vehicle. The inductor L3, which is in the collector circuit of the rf amplifier transistor, is tuned to two different frequencies. Capacitor C3 tunes L3 to the same frequency to which L2 is tuned. This is the frequency of the radio station being received. Capacitor C4 also tunes L3. This capacitor tunes L3 to the image frequency, a frequency other than the received frequency. The image frequency is the signal frequency (F_s) plus two times the i-f frequency (F_{i-f}) or $F_s + 2F_{i-f}$. In the standard American-made car radio, this will be equal to $F_s + 2 \times 262.5$ kHz. If the radio were tuned to 1000 kHz, the image frequency would appear at 1000 kHz $+ 2 \times 262.5$ kHz or 1000 kHz $+ 525$ kHz $= 1525$ kHz. The radio would respond to the 1525 kHz when it was tuned to 1000 kHz. On the crowded a-m broadcast band, this would produce chaos for the listener. The tuned circuit (C4 and L3) suppresses the image frequency and greatly improves the so-called image response of the radio. Without this image trap, the heterodyne image could easily interfere with the proper operation of the radio. The trap is parallel resonant at the image frequency. The purpose of a parallel resonant circuit is to offer a high impedance to its own resonant frequency, while offering a low impedance to all other frequencies. This arrangement allows the trap to pass the rf signal while blocking the image signal. A capacitive voltage divider couples the output from the rf amplifier to the input of the converter stage. Its function is to match the output impedance of the rf amplifier to the input impedance of the converter transistor. Not all car radios will use this voltage divider, however.

Choke coil L1 (Figs. 1-2 and 1-4) is one of those parts that seems out of place until its value and function are made known. The rf choke has a very low inductance. Because of this, L1 will have only a negligible inductive reactance at frequencies occupied by the a-m broadcast band. It will, of course, offer a higher reactance at higher frequencies ($X_L = 2\pi f L$). Noise signals from automobile ignitions and other sparking sources are in the form of pulses with an irregular waveshape. Such signals are extremely rich in high-frequency harmonics. The purpose of L1 is to suppress these high-frequency harmonics, thereby attenuating the noise pulses. It offers opposition to the noise pulse while passing the input signal virtually unaffected. Since car radios are prone to motor noise by the proximity of the auto ignition system, they almost universally incorporate this choke into the antenna circuit. Home radios almost never use such a choke.

Converter

A converter stage functions as both the local oscillator and the mixer. Using just one transistor is an economy measure. This stage must generate the local signal by operating as a vfo. It must also mix its own frequency with the incoming rf signal to produce the i-f signal. In reality, the converter will produce four signals at its output: the rf signal (F_s), the oscillator signal (F_o), and two new signals ($F_s + F_o$ and $F_o - F_s$). There are also a number of other combination signals present. However, these are usually too weak to be of importance. A parallel-resonant coil-capacitor tuned circuit picks off the $F_o - F_s$ signal while bypassing the others to ground via the power-supply decoupling capacitors. This tank circuit is tuned to the i-f frequency. The $F_o - F_s$, called simply the i-f signal, is inductively coupled to the secondary winding where it is then passed to the input of the i-f amplifier transistor.

Figs. 1-6 and 1-7 show two typical car radio converter stages. Fig. 1-6 is the older type converter using a pnp transistor. As in the rf amplifier stage, a resistor (R2 in this example) is used to stabilize the emitter circuit and to provide some isolation from the power supply. Notice that the value of the emitter resistor is approximately ten times the value of the emitter resistor in its respective rf amplifier (Fig. 1-2). Resistors R1 and R3 form a voltage divider network that provides dc bias to the base-emitter junction of the transistor. Fig. 1-7 illustrates a typical converter using an npn transistor. Except for the change in polarity with the required changes in circuit symmetry, this stage is similar to the pnp stage of Fig. 1-6.

In Fig. 1-6, the rf signal is coupled into the base circuit of the converter transistor by capacitor C1. This capacitor will pass the ac signal voltages as well as isolate the dc voltages in the two stages so that they cannot affect each other. This capacitor will usually have a value from close to .01 μF to as high as .08 μF.

Transformer T1 serves to pick out the proper mixer product and to couple it to the i-f amplifier stages. The oscillator feedback network—C2, C3, and C4—identifies the oscillator configuration as being a version of the famous Colpitts type. These capacitors also form the capacitive branch of the circuit that determines the frequency of oscillation. The coil L4 is the inductive branch. The frequency of oscillation will be $F_s + F_{i-f}$. Transformer T1 has minimal affect on the frequency of oscillation because it has a high impedance only at the i-f frequency. Of interest to technicians is the value of the dc bias voltage appearing between the base and emitter terminals of the transistor. In many sets, especially earlier pnp designs, this voltage will read close to zero. This is due to the fact that a vtvm or vom cannot follow the voltage changes caused by having the oscillator signal alternately add to and subtract from the bias voltage. The net result on a meter is an apparent indication of zero voltage. There are other means for checking the operation of the local oscillator. These will be discussed in a later chapter.

Figs. 1-8 and 1-9 show the direction of current flow directions in two types of converter stages. As

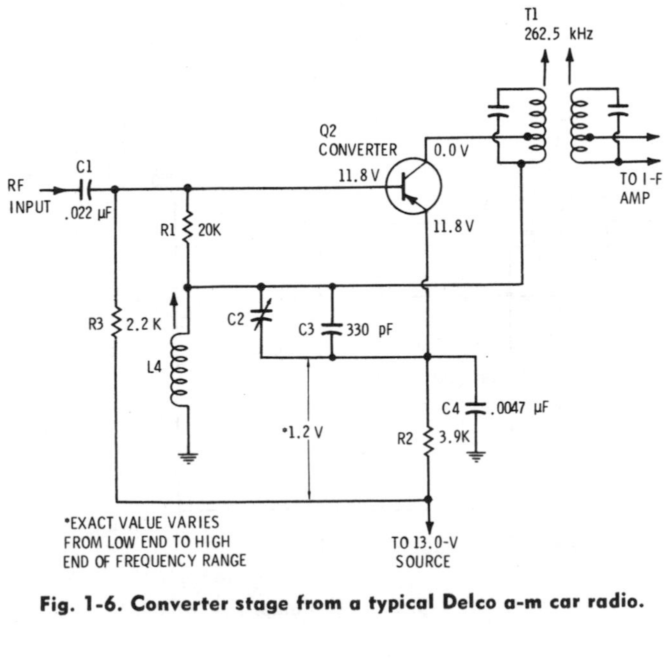

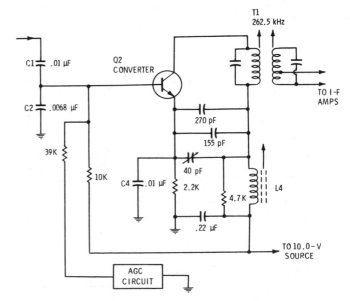

Fig. 1-6. Converter stage from a typical Delco a-m car radio.

Fig. 1-7. Typical npn converter stage.

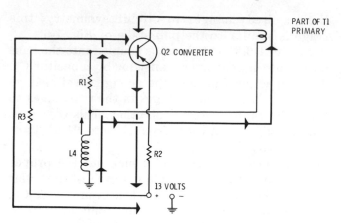

Fig. 1-8. Current flow (dc) for Fig. 1-6.

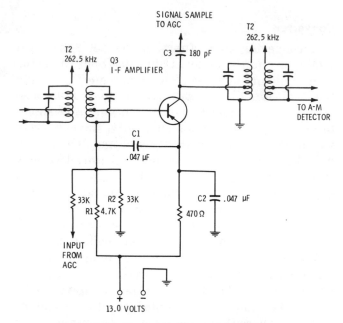

Fig. 1-10. Typical Delco pnp i-f amplifier.

in the rf amplifier stage or in any other amplifier stage, the current (electrons) flows against the arrow in the transistor symbol. Although not required for gaining a basic understanding of how radios work, an understanding of current flow is helpful when you troubleshoot the radio. Otherwise, voltage readings and their relationship to the proper operation of the radio may easily be misinterpreted.

I-F Amplifiers

Figs. 1-10 and 1-11 show the two basic types of i-f amplifiers used in car radio designs. In essence, these stages are merely fixed-tuned rf-style stages. The i-f amplifier has the highest gain of all stages in the radio. For this reason, the stage must be exceptionally stable. To limit feedback that could cause unwanted oscillation of this stage, the input and output i-f transformers are shielded by a metal housing or *can*. Decoupling, as well as higher gain, is provided by bypass capacitors C1 and C2.

Bias for the i-f amplifier transistor is supplied from two sources: the resistor voltage divider net-

work (consisting of R1 and R2) and the dc control voltage supplied by the agc circuit. The latter bias source is proportional to the strength of the received signal. When the radio is tuned to a strong station, this bias reduces the gain of the i-f and rf amplifier transistors. On weaker stations, the bias increases the gain of the two amplifiers. The affect of this is to reduce the loudness difference experienced by the listener as he tunes across the band encountering signals of widely varying strengths. In the pnp stages, the base of the transistor becomes more negative than the emitter—to increase

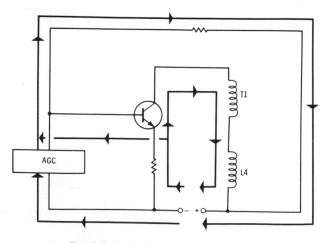

Fig. 1-9. Current flow (dc) for Fig. 1-7.

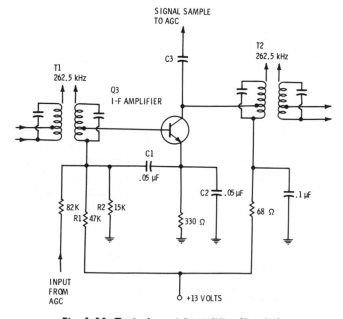

Fig. 1-11. Typical npn i-f amplifier (Bendix).

the stage gain. To reduce the stage gain, the agc circuit drives the base to a less negative voltage (as measured in relation to the emitter).

Selectivity in a radio is the property of rejecting all stations except that station to which the radio dial is tuned. Although no one has yet invented a way to receive one station while rejecting all others, the modern superhet approaches that ideal. The majority of receiver selectivity is a product of the i-f amplifier. The tuned i-f transformers have a high "Q" and are subcritically coupled. This produces a narrow selectivity curve or *bandpass*. Since a-m band channels are 10 kHz wide, the i-f amplifier must pass a range of frequencies up to 5 kHz either side of the center frequency. It must also attenuate signals outside of this range. Most car radio i-f amplifiers have passbands up to 10 or 12 kHz wide. This will allow them to pass the carrier and sidebands of one station while rejecting stations on adjacent channels. A few very novel a-m car radio designs have replaced the i-f transformers with ceramic filters.

The signal level sample used by the agc circuit to generate the dc control voltage is generally taken from the collector of the i-f amplifier stage. This is preferred because the i-f collector signal has a large enough value to be relatively free of noise and other components that could deteriorate the performance of the agc. It is also high enough to provide an effective agc, which might not be possible in a stage with a lower signal level. The sampling capacitor C3 will have a value in the 100-to-500 pF range with most of the capacitors being close to a value of 200 pF.

The i-f output transformer is usually a tapped-impedance resonant tank circuit type such as shown in Figs. 1-10 and 1-11. The input transformers, however, might be one of several popular designs. Fig. 1-12 shows three common types of i-f input transformers. In Fig. 1-12A is the tapped impedance type which is identical, except for impedance levels in some cases, to the i-f output transformer. Fig. 1-12B, however, shows a somewhat different type—a resonating capacitor is in series with the secondary winding. It not only resonates with the coil, but it also blocks the dc bias from flowing to ground via the transformer winding.

Fig. 1-12C illustrates a circuit used in one American radio and in many European and Japanese radios. Bendix began using this type of i-f transformer in their 1972 radios. In this circuit there are actually three windings, two of which are in a transformer configuration. The other is used as a

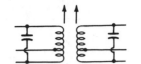

(A) Tapped impedance type.

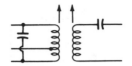

(B) Resonating capacitor in series with coil.

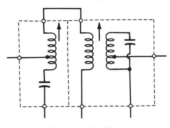

(C) Three-winding type.

Fig. 1-12. Coupling methods for an a-m i-f amplifier.

collector load for the i-f amplifier transistor or mixer stage.

AGC Section

Fig. 1-13 shows the block diagram of a typical agc section for a car radio. A sample of the signal is taken from the i-f amplifier and is fed to the agc circuit. Here it is converted by a rectifier to a dc voltage that is proportional to the strength of the station tuned in on the main dial. This voltage is filtered and decoupled to remove all traces of the ac signal before it is fed to the i-f and rf amplifiers. This is the dc voltage that determines the gain of these amplifiers.

The simplest style of agc is illustrated in Fig. 1-14. The circuit used with pnp transistor radios appears in Fig. 1-14A; that in Fig. 1-14B is for

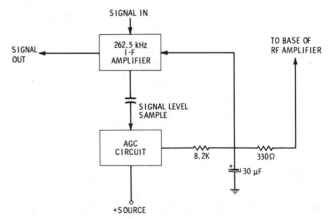

Fig. 1-13. Block diagram of a typical agc section.

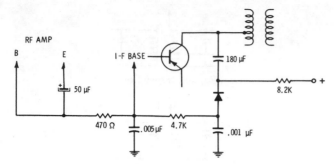

(A) *Circuit using a pnp transistor.*

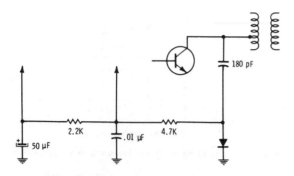

(B) *Circuit using an npn transistor.*

Fig. 1-14. Two typical a-m agc circuits.

use with npn radios. In either case, a single diode rectifier is used to transform the signal from the i-f stage into a dc voltage level that can control the amplifiers. Also, in both cases, there are capacitors to decouple residual i-f signal remaining on the agc control line. Should one of these capacitors become open (the electrolytic is the most frequent offender), the radio will oscillate as it is tuned across the band. The agc control line acts as a path for positive feedback. This type of defect is identifiable because it is tunable, that is, the *squeal* will vary in pitch as the radio is tuned across the dial. Between stations there will be little sound produced by the oscillation, because there is no signal for it to heterodyne against. As a station is approached, however, a high-pitched whistle is produced. This whistle reduces in pitch as you tune toward the center of the station. When the radio is tuned to the exact center of the station, the whistle disappears. This is called *zero beat*. When the difference between the two signals is zero, then the heterodyne output will also be zero.

In circuits similar to that in Fig. 1-14A, the level of the dc control voltage is close to the power-supply voltage. In these sets, the agc voltage is algebraically added to the power-supply voltage. The circuit in Fig. 1-14B, however, generates its own control voltage with no assistance from the power supply.

A variation on this circuit used by Delco for many years is shown in Fig. 1-15. This is the *voltage-doubler* or *two-diode* agc circuit. This type of circuit allegedly offers a wider dynamic agc range than does the single diode circuit used by others.

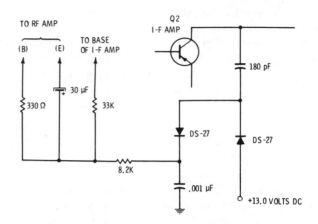

Fig. 1-15. Delco two-diode agc circuit.

Until 1971, Delco used their own Type DS-27 germanium diode in this circuit. In 1971, however, they switched to a silicon diode.

Detector

Before the listener can enjoy the radio program, the signal must be detected. The human ear cannot respond to the high-frequency variations amplified by the i-f amplifier stage. The incoming audio signal, which the human ear can respond to, is riding on the high-frequency carrier through the i-f section. The detector removes the carrier and extracts the audio signal so that it can be further amplified in the audio frequency (af) stages before being sent to the speaker. Although the mechanics of modulation are too complex to be treated here, it can be noted that the audio is extracted by rectifying the i-f signal. Since a rectifier is a nonlinar element, this causes the carrier to beat together with its sidebands to produce a difference signal that is the audio. This heterodyning is the reason why some people call the audio detector the *second detector*, while the converter is often called the *first detector*. Two typical car radio detector circuits are shown in Fig. 1-16. In Fig. 1-16A, the signal is fed to a simple diode. The circuit in Fig. 1-16B is a type of detector that uses dc from the power supply to bias the diode. This effectively gives the diode a higher impedance load so that it can develop a higher output voltage. Of the two types, the simple diode of Fig. 1-16A is the more common.

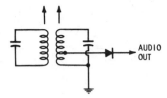

(A) Simple diode circuit.

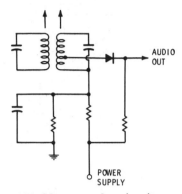

(B) More complex circuit.

Fig. 1-16. Detector circuits for a-m radios.

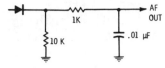

(A) Standard style.

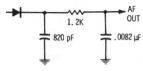

(B) Pi section.

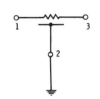

(C) Schematic symbol.

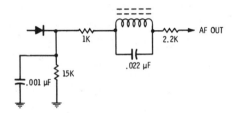

(D) Backward L-section with a parallel trap.

Fig. 1-17. Tweet-filter circuits.

Filters

Heterodynes from adjacent stations (10 kHz away) can interfere with normal reception on the crowded airwaves. To help reduce the level of this interference, modern car radios incorporate a 10-kHz filter (called either a *whistle* or *tweet filter*) in the circuit following the detector. Several such filters are shown in Fig. 1-17. One of the standard styles is shown in Fig. 1-17A. It consists of a 10K ohm load resistor followed by a RC L-section low-pass filter network. This circuit passes only those signals in the audio range under 5 kHz. Audio frequencies above 5 kHz are attenuated. A pi-section variation of this circuit is shown in Fig. 1-17B. Its operation is similar to that of the L-section filter in the previous example. In some of the car radios, there are tweet filters built into a ceramic package designed for printed-circuit mounting. Although they are either L-section or pi-section circuits, they have a different type of schematic symbol. This symbol is shown in Fig. 1-17C as an underscored resistor. That is, a line is drawn underneath the resistor.

Becoming increasingly popular with the availability of small, low-cost inductors of suitable value is the type of tweet filter shown in Fig. 1-17D. This design uses an RC *backward L-section* to feed a parallel-resonant 10-kHz LC trap. This trap is usually fixed rather than adjustable. The trap will block its resonant frequency while passing all others. The L-section preceding the trap attenuates those signals above 5 kHz, which the trap would otherwise permit to pass.

Decoupling

General voltage distribution and decoupling in the standard a-m radio is shown in Fig. 1-18. The

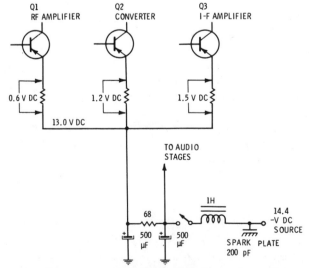

Fig. 1-18. General voltage distribution and decoupling.

input from the car battery is approximately 14 volts. Noise pulses (rf) from the ignition system can enter the radio via the power lead and cause interference. To suppress these pulses, there is an iron-core choke coil and two capacitors. One of these input capacitors is a standard high capacitance, low-voltage electrolytic. The other is a less familiar type called a *spark plate*. This capacitor generally has a capacitance in the 200-pF range. It consists of two pieces of copper foil glued to opposite sides of a piece of fishpaper or other insulating material. One side of this sandwich is soldered directly to the radio chassis at a point close to where the power lead enters the set. The other side is soldered to the power lead.

ICs

With the rapid advances in integrated-circuit (IC) technology, it was only natural to expect someone to come with up an IC to replace all of the semiconductor devices normally found in the front-end of an a-m radio. This includes the rf amplifier, converter, i-f amplifier and agc. Fig. 1-19 shows the circuit of such a radio introduced on a limited production basis by Delco Electronics in 1972. The IC has been designated as Type DM-20. It comes in the 14-pin dual in-line package. Notice

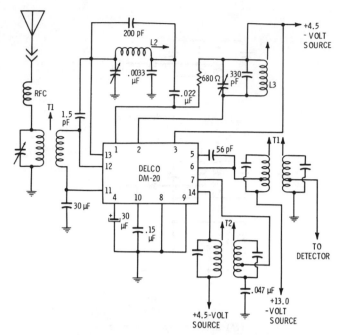

Fig. 1-19. Delco "one IC" a-m car radio.

that this circuit contains most of the parts normally found in a car radio. It eliminates the bias and certain other dc components used in a regular radio and can be built into a space considerably smaller than the normal radio.

Chapter 2

Audio Section

The audio amplifier stages are the most important factor in determining the user's enjoyment of his car audio system. It is in these stages that many distortion problems occur. Also, it is these stages which determine both frequency response and output power of the system.

FREQUENCY RESPONSE

It is impossible to use one frequency-response characteristic as universal among all automotive electronic equipment. The typical frequency response may be quite varied among the various types of equipment. In a simple a-m radio there is little need for a frequency response greater than about 5 kHz. This is due to the fact that many a-m broadcast stations are limited in audio response. Since there may be no recoverable program material above 5 kHz, but there will be other forms of undesirable interference in this range, it is actually a disadvantage to have an a-m radio with a wideband audio amplifier. However, fm broadcasters enjoy a wider latitude of the audio spectrum. These stations are permitted to transmit audio frequencies up to 15 kHz. In fact, not only are the higher frequencies transmitted, they are actually given a degree of pre-emphasis in order to improve the signal-to-noise ratio at the receiver. An fm car radio, therefore, may easily have a frequency response wide enough to include frequencies up to 15 kHz. Since most modern fm sets also include an a-m band, it is desirable to be able to reduce the audio bandwidth on a-m and increase it on fm. In some sets this is accomplished by the regular tone-control circuitry. The user is

expected to adjust the control to give the most pleasing effect. In other sets, the audio amplifiers are designed to offer the 15-kHz fm response characteristic. The a-m response is limited by incorporating an RC low-pass filter between the a-m detector and the audio input. In certain other designs the requirement is handled either by a compromise response of around 8 kHz or by ignoring the problem altogether.

POWER

For the fan who loves super-power audio systems, it may come as quite a surprise to learn that car radio and tape players seldom produce more than a few watts (continuous) per channel. In fact, some of the lower-priced models offer something less than one watt of power. Even the most expensive sets will not offer much more than ten watts per-channel maximum, and most American car radios are rated closer to five watts.

FEEDBACK

Negative feedback plays an important part in automotive electronic designs. Fig. 2-1 shows two very common feedback circuits. In Fig. 2-1A, we see what is called the *second collector to first emitter* circuit. Fig. 2-1B is called the *second emitter to first base* circuit. In some cases you will find that Fig. 2-1A is used between two stages in the radio, while Fig. 2-1B is being used simultaneously—but somewhere else in the radio. Combination feedback methods are very common in most brands of car radios.

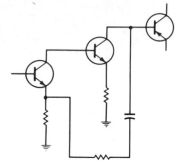

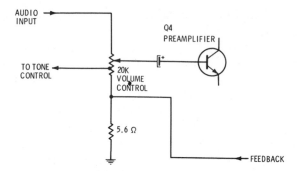

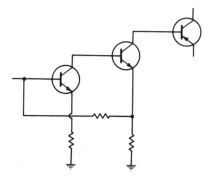

(A) Second collector to first emitter circuit.

Fig. 2-3. Typical volume control circuit.

(B) Second emitter to first base circuit.

Fig. 2-1. Two common feedback methods employed in audio-amplifier sections.

AUDIO STAGES

Fig. 2-2 shows the block diagram of an audio amplifier section. The signal from the i-f amplifier is fed to either a simple a-m (diode) detector or one of the more complex fm detectors. The detected audio signal is fed to the preamplifier stage via a volume control and a variable tone-shaping

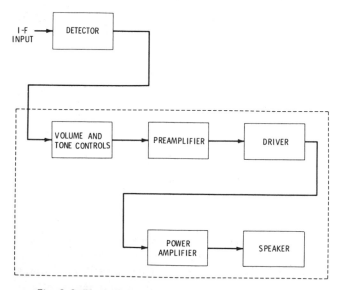

Fig. 2-2. Block diagram of a typical audio section in a car radio.

circuit. The preamplifier strengthens the signal and passes it on to the driver stage. The driver amplifier is frequently another voltage-amplifier stage. In some designs, however, it is also a minor power amplifier. The purpose of the driver stage is to further develop the audio signal so that it is strong enough to drive the power-amplifier transistor. The power amplifier supplies the audio power required by the speaker. These stages almost universally contain larger and more powerful transistors than the preamplifier and driver stages.

Volume and Tone Controls

The input side of the audio section usually contains the volume control. Most American car radios use a circuit similar to the Delco circuit shown in Fig. 2-3. Audio is taken from the control wiper terminal to the audio preamplifier input via a coupling capacitor. Its function is to isolate the control from the preamplifier bias network. Feedback from the collector of the output transistor is frequently applied to this circuit.

Normally, tone controls in car radios are of the treble rolloff variety. An example of this is shown in Fig. 2-4 which is also from a Delco design. The setting of the tone potentiometer determines the degree and frequency characteristics of the rolloff curve. Only a very few car radios or tape players

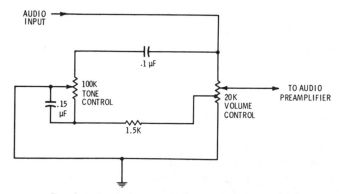

Fig. 2-4. Typical tone and volume control circuit.

use the negative feedback "Baxandall" tone-control circuit.

Fig. 2-5 shows the complete control section for one channel of a stereo audio section. The relative position of the balance control wiper determines the amplitude of the signals at the respective inputs. When the balance control is set all the way toward one channel, the signal line to the other channel will be shorted to ground, while the signal in the live channel will be only slightly attenuated.

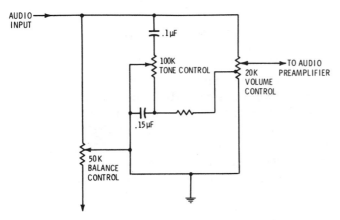

Fig. 2-5. Typical audio control circuit featuring volume, tone, and balance controls.

Preamplifiers

Fig. 2-6 illustrates one of the earliest types of solid-state preamplifier stages. This circuit functions as both driver and preamplifier. The input signal from the volume control is coupled by a capacitor to the base terminal of Q4. The output signal is coupled to the base of the power-amplifier transistor by an interstage transformer, much in the same manner as previous vacuum-tube designs. The bias for these stages is usually class-A. Decoupling is accomplished by high-value electrolytic capacitors. These capacitors are generally part of a multisection filter capacitor.

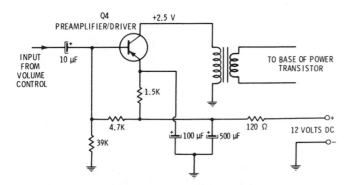

Fig. 2-6. An early-model solid-state preamplifier.

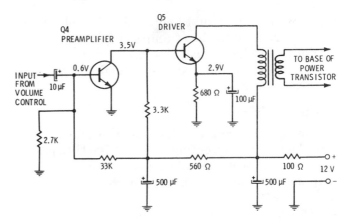

Fig. 2-7. Two-stage preamplifier.

A significant improvement in gain is offered by the preamplifier circuit shown in Fig. 2-7, which uses two direct-coupled transistors. Transistor Q4 acts as the preamplifier while Q5 functions as the driver stage. Note that the collector voltage at Q4 is the same as the base voltage of Q5. This allows the elimination of coupling devices such as capacitors and transformers. The input signal applied to the base of Q4 causes the collector voltage to vary. These variations are read by the driver transistor as an ac input signal—then Q5 further amplifies this signal and couples it to the power amplifier through an interstage transformer.

Fig. 2-8 shows an obsolete preamplifier which enjoyed only brief popularity. It is a hybrid design using both a transistor and a vacuum tube. When these circuits were being used, the auto radio field was in a transition period between the earlier vacuum-tube technology and the newer all solid-state technology. In those days, most car radios used special vacuum tubes that could operate satisfac-

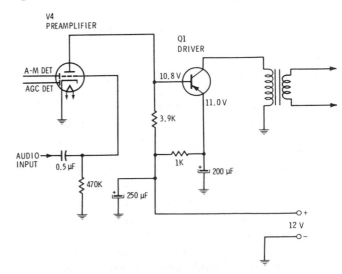

Fig. 2-8. Hybrid tube/transistor preamplifier.

torily with only 10 or 12 volts on the anode. These tubes were used in the rf amplifier, converter, and i-f amplifier circuits because high-frequency transistors were still too expensive, and for practical purposes, untried.

Power Amplifiers

The power amplifier develops the audio signal into the strong current needed to drive the speaker voice coil. Power amplifiers are generally current amplifiers, because of the low impedance levels associated with speaker systems. Fig. 2-9 shows the schematic of a typical early solid-state power amplifier. This circuit uses a pnp germanium transistor. The bias network contains a thermally sensitive resistor (thermister) to provide some degree of temperature stability. In more modern designs, a solid-state diode is used in this function. The low-value resistor in the emitter circuit is called a fusible resistor. Its function is two-fold. First, since it is unbypassed it offers a small amount of negative feedback. Due to its small value it appears to be insignificant, but many car radios have been known to be particularly sensitive to changes in the value of the fusible resistor.

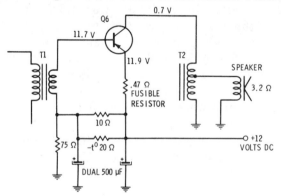

Fig. 2-9. Typical early-model solid-state power amplifier.

Typical values for these parts run from approximately 0.20 to 1.2 ohms. Although substitutions are sometimes permissible, do not use a replacement that is too far from the original value. It is a matter of percentages; if you replace a 0.22 ohm with a 0.47 ohm, you will change the value more than 100%. The second function of the fusible resistor, as its name implies, is fusing. Should the output transistor become shorted, the fusible resistor is supposed to be destroyed by the excess current flow. Although this cannot help the transistor, it does offer some protection to the other power-amplifier parts and the power supply. In cases where the fusible resistor fails to open, secondary damage to the radio can be extensive.

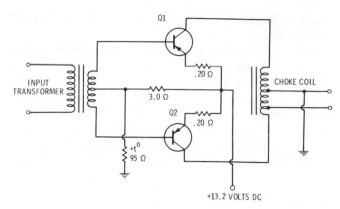

Fig. 2-10. Standard push-pull power amplifier.

Performance improvements can be realized by the use of push-pull audio power amplifiers. These circuits fall into several basic categories: standard push-pull, complementary symmetry push-pull, and totem pole push-pull. There are also several other variations on the push-pull theme, but these had only a limited life span in car radio design. Fig. 2-10 is a standard push-pull amplifier. This particular circuit is from a Philips radio which was made for Chrysler. Once again we see the use of pnp germanium transistors. The interstage (input) transformer is of the center-tapped style usually associated with push-pull amplifier circuits. The output circuit, however, is a push-pull version of an output choke coil. However, in some radios this may be a transformer rather than a choke. In any solid-state push-pull amplifier, the transistors must be given a slight forward-bias in order to prevent crossover distortion. This type of distortion occurs as the input signal approaches the zero axis. It is due to the nature of performance of transistors at low signal levels.

Figs. 2-11 and 2-12 show a variation on the normal push-pull theme. In these circuits the speaker voice coil is used as the load for the output transistors. The circuit in Fig. 2-11 uses a 20-ohm center-tapped speaker. Although this speaker is now

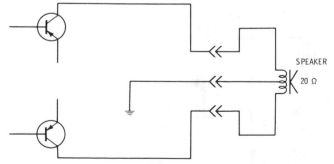

Fig. 2-11. Output of a push-pull amplifier using a 20-ohm center-tapped speaker as the load.

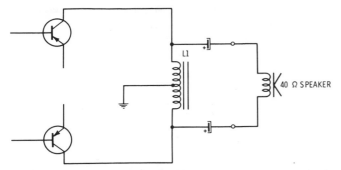

Fig. 2-12. Example showing the use of a 40-ohm speaker load.

hard to locate, an adequate substitute may be fashioned from a universal multi-impedance speaker. These speakers usually have two 8- to 10-ohm voice coils that can be used in series, parallel, or individually to nominally cover the 4–20 ohm range. Phasing of the two windings, in this case, is critical and must be determined experimentally by the cut-and-try method. Fig. 2-12 shows a circuit that uses a 40-ohm speaker. In this case, it is actually necessary to order a 40-ohm speaker.

One of the requirements for push-pull amplification is that one transistor must operate over one-half of the input cycle, while the other transistor operates over the other half. In the standard push-pull circuit of Fig. 2-10, this phase inversion is accomplished by the use of a center-tapped transformer. If the center tap is considered common,

the signal at the extreme end of one side of the secondary winding is 180° out of phase with the signal at the opposite extreme. This will drive one transistor into conduction as the other is turned off. The complementary-symmetry configuration in Fig. 2-13 uses the polarity differences between npn and pnp transistors to accomplish phase inversion. The npn transistor Q3 will conduct as the base voltage becomes more positive than the emitter. And since Q4 is a pnp transistor, it will conduct when the base voltage becomes less positive than the emitter. Because of this action, Q3 will operate (conduct) on the positive half-cycle of the input signal, while Q4 will operate on the negative half. The audio is routed to the speaker through an electrolytic capacitor. Typical values for the speaker capacitor will normally be in the range of 300 to 2000 μF. The diode used in this circuit gives the transistors a slight forward-bias in order to reduce crossover distortion.

The totem pole push-pull amplifiers have been very popular with Japanese manufacturers. An example of a typical Japanese totem pole power amplifier is shown in Fig. 2-14. In this circuit both output transistors are pnp. If a transistor should become defective, most manufacturers recommend replacement of both transistors so that a matched pair can be inserted. The output coupling of the totem pole is almost identical to that of the com-

Fig. 2-13. Example of complementary symmetry push-pull.

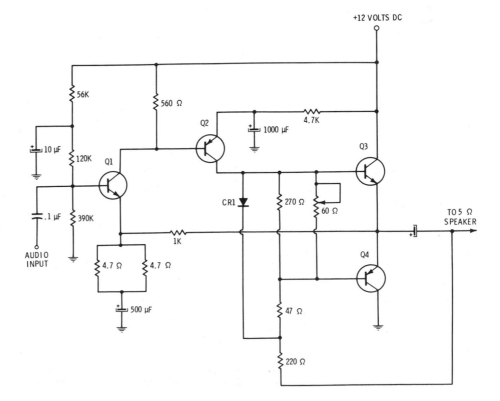

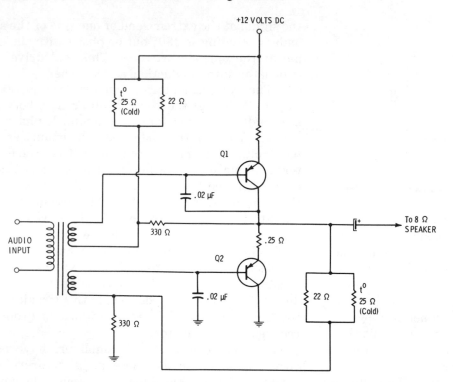

Fig. 2-14. Totem pole push-pull amplifier section.

plementary circuit. The input side of the amplifier is the distinguishing part. Phase inversion occurs by using a specially designed interstage transformer that has two secondary windings. The two windings are connected to their respective base terminals in opposite "sense" so that there will be a 180° difference between the two signals. Small disc ceramic capacitors are connected between the output transistor base and collector terminals to suppress rf oscillations that could occur.

TROUBLESHOOTING THE AUDIO SECTION

Fig. 2-15 shows a complete Motorola audio section. Although this particular circuit is of more recent design, it is a direct descendent of earlier

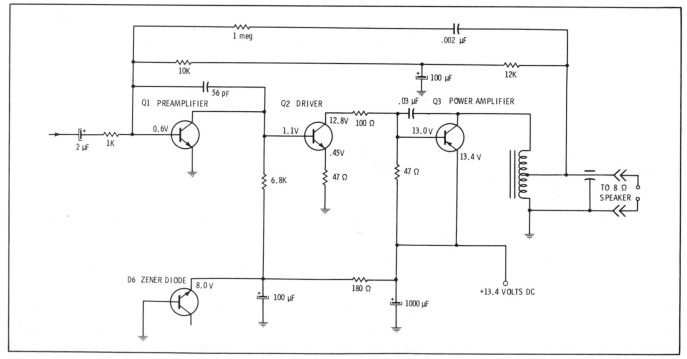

Fig. 2-15. Complete Motorola audio section.

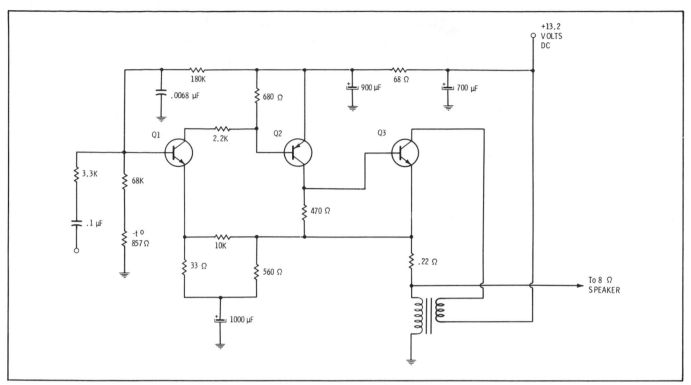

Fig. 2-16. Recent Bendix audio-amplifier design.

designs by the same manufacturer. In troubleshooting these direct-coupled stages, it must be remembered that any one defect in the audio section will affect the dc conditions throughout the amplifier. For example, should Q2 become shorted (collector to emitter), the base voltage of the output transistor will reduce. Since the output transistor is a pnp, the forward-bias on Q3 will increase by whatever voltage is removed from the base. Such a condition will drive Q3 into saturation and make it appear shorted. Transistor Q1 can also affect the output transistor. If it ceases to conduct, its collector voltage will rise because of the decreased voltage drop across the 6.8K resistor. This saturates Q2, causing it to draw excessive collector current. With an increase in collector current, Q2 will have a considerable decrease in collector voltage. This reduces the Q3 base voltage (increasing forward-bias) to a point where Q3 is saturated and appears shorted. A collector-to-emitter short at Q1 also shorts the base of Q2 to ground. This causes Q2, an npn transistor, to cut off. Since almost zero collector current will flow in Q2 under these conditions, the base voltage of Q3 will rise to a point where Q3 is cut off.

Fig. 2-16 is a recent audio-amplifier design by Bendix. An increase in the collector current of transistor Q2 will automatically increase the conduction of Q3. Since Q2 is a pnp device, its collector current increases when its base voltage becomes lower (less positive) than its emitter voltage. This voltage level for Q2 is a function of the collector current drawn by the preamplifier transistor Q1. As Q1 increases conduction, Q2 will also increase conduction. With increased current levels flowing in the Q2 collector circuit, there will be a greater voltage impressed across the Q2 collector resistor. It is this voltage that is used to control the conduction of the npn output transistor Q3. Notice that in this circuit the output incorporates a transformer, rather than a simple choke. This is necessary in order to isolate the high positive voltage on the collector of Q3 from the grounded speaker circuit. A certain amount of negative feedback is gained by having both the collector and emitter windings on the output transformer.

There have been two general areas of trouble in these circuits. One is failure of the output transistor. Most car radio output transistors found defective are shorted. In audio amplifiers such as Fig. 2-16, however, the npn output transistors are often the victim of a base-to-emitter open condition. In these situations, the Q3 base voltage will be almost as high as the collector voltage. Another area of fault is the 1000-μF decoupling capacitor. The electrolytics will occasionally open, causing low volume and distortion. When the capacitor fails in this manner, the relative dc levels are not affected.

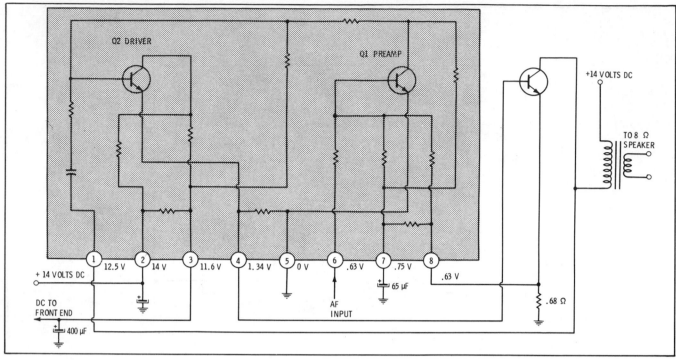

Fig. 2-17. A Philco PEC design.

NEW DESIGNS

Although most car radios have used regular discrete components in the audio preamplifier and driver stages, Delco and Philco have elected to use Packaged Electronic Component (PEC) audio systems. In these circuits the preamplifier and driver circuitry, including the transistors, are housed in either epoxy or ceramic modules soldered to the printed-circuit board. Fig. 2-17 shows the PEC design used by Philco in some of the late-model Ford a-m radios. High-value electrolytic capacitors and the power transistor are external to the package. The Delco modules, Types DM-8 and DM-28, are similar in concept, if not in design and appearance.

Motorola has taken a different path in the design of the audio stage. Fig. 2-18 shows a typical

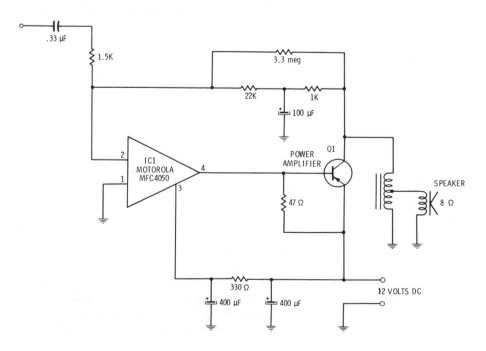

Fig. 2-18. Motorola integrated-circuit audio section.

Motorola audio section using a tiny integrated circuit (MFC4050). Preamplifier and driver stages are housed inside a plastic case less than one-half inch in its greatest dimension. This circuit is the utmost in simplicity. It has only four terminals: input, output, common (signal and dc on one terminal), and positive voltage source. The output terminal is directly coupled to the base of the power transistor. This power transistor is a pnp germanium type that has enjoyed long popularity in Motorola car radio designs. An external feedback network shapes the tonal characteristics of the overall circuit.

Failure of the MFC4050 can cause either saturation or cutoff of the output transistor. Should the output transistor be saturated (dc readings such as collector voltage and collector current will make it appear shorted), try shorting the output transistor base and emitter terminals together to determine the faulty component. If the collector current drops to zero when this is done, it proves that the transistor base junction is still capable of controlling the collector current. In this case, the finger of suspicion should fall on the MFC4050 IC. If, on the other hand, the collector current fails to drop appreciably when the base and emitter terminals are shorted together, you may safely assume that the transistor is shorted. In cases where the output is cut off (almost zero collector current), connect a resistor (approximately 100 ohms) between the output transistor base terminal and ground. If this causes the output transistor to begin conducting, then the IC is probably open. IC terminal voltages offer a guide to some defects but cannot be relied upon to tell the final story in all situations.

Chapter 3

FM—From RF Amplifier to Detector

Car radios with fm became a practical reality in the early sixties with the advent of low cost, high-frequency transistors and other solid-state devices. Although the performance of those early all transistor sets was poor compared to what is available today, they were considerably better than the tube models. Noise and frequency drift were so common in tube designs that many manufacturers simply refused to offer fm car radios. The fm car radio of today, however, is capable of equaling the performance of all but the very best home stereo receivers.

BLOCK DIAGRAM

A block diagram for an fm car radio is essentially the same as that for an a-m radio; both utilize a superhet. There are, however, certain differences worthy of note. One is the heterodyning circuitry. Most a-m car radios use a single converter transistor for both local oscillator and mixer stage functions. Most fm car radios, on the other hand, use separate oscillator and mixer transistors. The average a-m radio uses only one stage of i-f amplification. Almost all fm sets, however, have at least three i-f amplifier stages, with some using as many as five. The last stage in an fm i-f amplifier is usually a limiter. This is one reason for the seemingly excessive number of i-f amplifiers—the signal must be built up to a point where it can drive the limiter properly. The detector in an a-m radio is nothing more than a simple one-diode envelope detector. However, detection is more involved, and the detector circuits more complex. Fig. 3-1 is a photograph of a late-model Delco fm car radio receiver. Notice that compared to home receivers of comparable specifications, this type of radio seems to have few controls for the user to adjust. Space is so severely limited that designers must either eliminate certain features or make them entirely automatic. There is, for example, no switch to allow the user to turn off the afc (automatic frequency control). The afc must simply operate at all times.

RF AMPLIFIER

Fig. 3-2 shows the rf amplifier stage from an early Delco fm radio. This stage uses a pnp germanium transistor. Most recent sets, however, are using npn silicon transistors because they offer better performance. This stage is the common-base configuration which is conventional in fm rf amplifier design. Tube circuit analogy for this stage would be a grounded-grid amplifier. One reason why so many designers choose the common-base configuration is that the effective junction capacitance of the transistor is reduced to a point where little or no neutralization is required. Since an fm rf amplifier must cover a relatively wide frequency range, located in a part of the radio spectrum where a little extra capacitance is a large percentage of the total, it is advisable to eliminate the neutralization circuitry as much as possible. The common-base configuration offers the best performance for the money in fm rf amplifiers using bipolar transistors. Notice that the bias network keeps the transistor at a dc level above ground. A bypass capacitor on the base is used to shunt the ac signal voltages to ground.

Signal input to the common-base stage is on the emitter terminal. A small-value capacitor (2 pF)

Fig. 3-1. Photograph of a late-model fm car radio.

from the resonant tank circuit couples the signal to the emitter and isolates the tank from the emitter dc potential. The antenna is matched to the tank circuit by connecting it to a low-impedance tap on the tank coil. In automobile radios, the coil is usually the circuit element varied when the radio is tuned. However, in the circuit of Fig. 3-2, there is a variable capacitor gang used for this purpose. Since the output tank circuit is located at the collector terminal of the pnp transistor with reference to ground, the inductor in the tank circuit can also be used as a dc ground return path. The collector circuit of the rf amplifier is isolated from the base of the mixer by a 2-pF capacitor. The high-frequency signals are kept out of power supply by .002-μF ceramic feedthrough capacitors. These are used in preference to other types of capacitors because of their superior performance in the vhf range. The leads on other types of capacitors often contain excessive inductance in the vhf range. Ferrite sleeve beads are often placed over the power-supply leads at the external connection to the by-

pass capacitors. These ferrite beads limit the extent of the magnetic field surrounding the wires and thereby prevent feedback from spurious radiation. If unchecked, this radiation could cause the radio to oscillate.

An npn bipolar transistor used in an fm rf amplifier circuit is illustrated in Fig. 3-3. This circuit is from one of the Bendix car radios made for Ford. This style of circuit has become more or less standard in modern fm car radios. The main difference in configuration between the pnp and npn stages is the applied dc polarity. Considering both to be negative ground systems, the npn transistor will have positive supply voltage fed to the collector through the tuning coil while the collector of a pnp transistor would be at dc ground.

In the 1972 Ford fm models, Bendix switched to the use of a metal-oxide semiconductor field-effect transistor (MOSFET) in the rf amplifier. A MOSFET has considerably better rf amplifier characteristics than do bipolar variety transistors. The MOSFET performance equals that of vacuum tubes without generating any of the more serious disadvantages of vacuum tubes. Cross modulation and other overload problems are lessened to a substantial degree by the use of the MOSFET. The Bendix MOSFET fm rf amplifier circuit is shown in Fig. 3-4. The particular device chosen for this circuit is one of the dual gate, diode-protected types. Nonprotected MOSFET transistors are subject to destruction by static charges that can build up on the technician's hands or even his tools. Extreme care must be exercised in the handling of nonprotected MOSFETs. To protect against static damage, the nonprotected MOSFETs come pack-

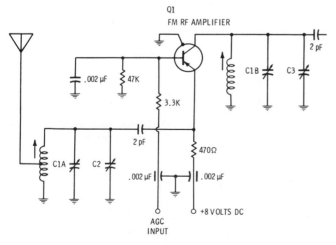

Fig. 3-2. An rf amplifier stage from an early Delco fm radio.

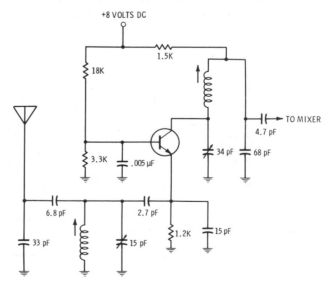

Fig. 3-3. An npn rf amplifier from a Bendix car radio.

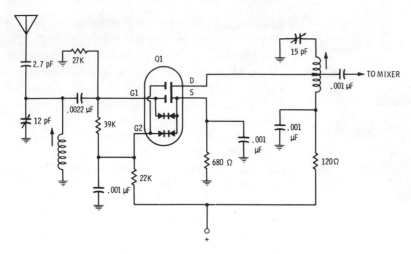

Fig. 3-4. A Bendix MOSFET fm rf amplifier.

aged with a shorting ring that binds all the leads together. This ring is cut off after the transistor has been installed in the circuit. The interelement diodes serve as a safe discharge path for static charges—they shunt the high-voltage transients around the delicate gate insulation.

LOCAL OSCILLATOR

Fig. 3-5 shows a typical local oscillator from an fm car radio (Motorola model 1VW2109 made for Volkswagen). This local oscillator, as well as most other fm local oscillators, is a common-base configuration. A 3.3-pF capacitor between the collector and emitter terminals of the transistor serves to provide the positive feedback needed for oscillation.

Automatic Frequency Control

One interesting point in these circuits is the variable capacitance diode (varactor) used for auto-matic frequency control (afc). A varactor has the ability to change its junction capacitance with changes in the reverse bias voltage level. An error correction signal in the form of a dc voltage is generated by the fm detector whenever the oscillator drifts off frequency. This error voltage varies the capacitance of the diode to change the frequency of the oscillator. When the local oscillator is pulled back on frequency, the dc error signal disappears. In this way, the afc causes the radio to remain perfectly tuned to the center of the received station signal. If it were not for afc, the drift inherent in the vhf variable-frequency oscillator would cause the received signal to drift intolerably about the correct spot on the dial. The afc causes the fm receiver to appear to grab the station as the dial is tuned toward its position in the band. This gives a characteristic *thump* as the radio is tuned to a station. If the control exhibited by the afc loop is too tight, the tuning section of the radio is considered too "broad." This occurs because the afc is

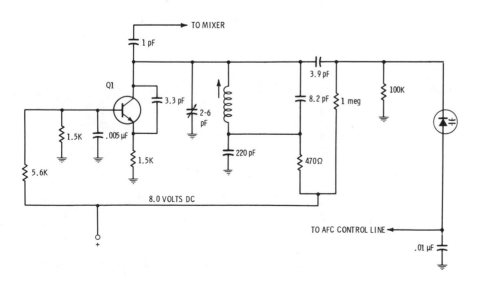

Fig. 3-5. Typical local oscillator from an fm car radio.

controlling the oscillator signal for too great a distance across the dial.

Another possible defect in afc design is a control loop that is too loose. Since most of the electrical parameters in an automobile tend to change with changing conditions, the fm radio with a weak control loop may tend to jump into and out of afc lock as the car is driven along. Some of the variables that could cause this problem can be eliminated. Voltage variations, for example, can be lessened by the use of a regulated power supply. The most common form of regulation is the zener diode. In any event, a properly designed afc loop can make all the difference in the world to the user, even though he may not even be aware of its existence.

Fig. 3-6 shows a partial schematic of an afc loop. The error signal is developed by the fm detector. This is a dc voltage level applied through an RC network to the varactor diode in the fm local oscillator. Part of the function of the RC network is to bring the control voltage level to the exact range required by the diode for smooth operation. The capacitors in this network serve to decouple the

control loop. Since the afc control loop is connected to several stages in the cascade chain, it is possible for ac signal feedback to occur. The capacitors in the afc line decouple any signal voltages that could cause trouble, and they also tend to keep the voltage level on the afc line constant.

MIXER

In a superheterodyne radio receiver, it is necessary to beat the local oscillator signal against the rf amplifier signal in order to produce a difference frequency. This frequency, called the intermediate frequency or simply i-f, is easier to handle than the original rf signal. If you join two signals together in an amplifier stage that is perfectly linear, the circuit will simply amplify both signals with no mixing action (no difference frequency). In a properly designed mixer stage, there must be a certain degree of nonlinearity so that mixing can occur. In the npn mixer stage of Fig. 3-7, both rf and local oscillator signals are applied to the base of the mixer transistor. In other designs, the rf signal is applied to the base while the local oscillator signal is applied to the emitter. In mixer circuits using a dual-gate MOSFET, the rf signal is generally applied to gate No. 1 and the oscillator to gate No. 2. In all car radios, the i-f frequency is picked off the collector by a resonant transformer circuit. The standard fm i-f is 10.7 MHz. A few foreign types, however, can be found using either 4.5 MHz or 6.5 MHz. Some will be double-conversion types using 10.7 MHz as the high i-f and one of the other two frequencies as the low i-f. Many mixer designs incorporate a series tuned i-f trap connected between the base and emitter terminals of the transistor in the mixer stage. This trap prevents certain intermodulation problems while simultaneously providing higher mixer gain at the i-f.

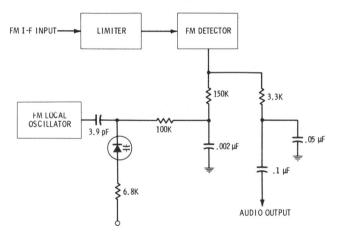

Fig. 3-6. Partial schematic of an afc loop.

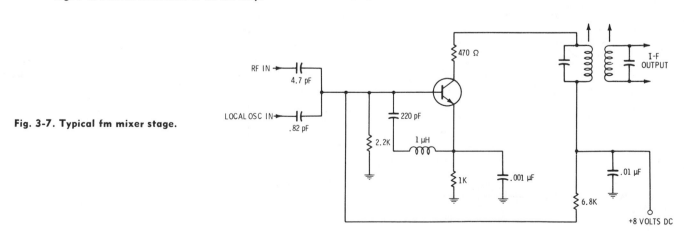

Fig. 3-7. Typical fm mixer stage.

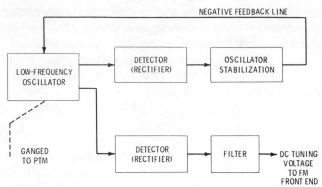

Fig. 3-8. Block diagram of a tuning voltage generator
and regulator.

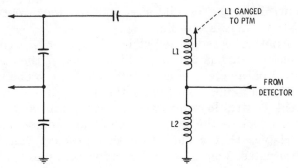

Fig. 3-9. A variable inductive voltage divider.

VARACTORS

In 1972, Philco introduced a radical new style of fm car radio. It has been stated previously that varactor diodes automatically retune the local oscillator in response to dc voltage commands sent from the fm detector. Since varactors can be used to easily tune a vhf tank circuit, it seemed only natural that someone would use them to tune the entire fm front end. One of the chief problems facing such a design was control of the tuning voltage. Any change in the tuning voltage, whether desired or accidental, will cause the radio to shift frequency. Fig. 3-8 shows the circuitry used by Philco to limit spurious tuning voltage excursions. A low-frequency oscillator generates the source voltage needed for tuning. A rectifier and filter circuit converts the ac oscillations into the pure dc needed by the varactor-controlled front-end. An-

other rectifier and a control amplifier for oscillator stabilization is used in a negative dc feedback system to keep the ac level constant. The varactor front end needs a dc voltage that varies from approximately .7 volt dc to 7 volts dc. The output of the low-frequency oscillator would be constant under normal circumstances. In the Philco circuit, a pair of inductors are used (Fig. 3-9) as a variable ac voltage divider to provide a controlled but variable signal level for the rectifier. These two inductors are series connected and form the inductive branch of the low-frequency oscillator resonant tank circuit. The variable inductor L1 is ganged to the core bar in the main permeability tuning mechanism (PTM). The lower coil L2 is fixed. As the frequency of the low-frequency oscillator is varied, the relative reactance of the two coils also changes. The value of the ac voltage appearing across L2 changes as the position of the L1 slug changes. This varies the dc output from the detector and tunes the fm front end.

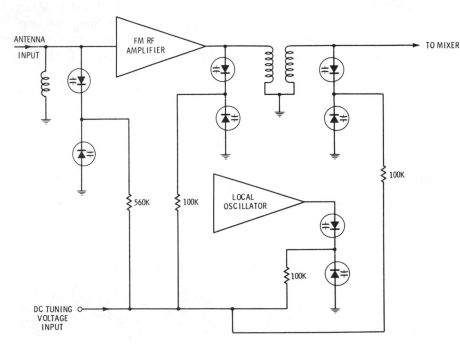

Fig. 3-10. Partial schematic of the tuning circuitry from a Philco radio.

Fig. 3-10 shows a partial schematic of the Philco tuning circuitry. The tuning varactors are, in reality, double diodes rather than the single diode types used in most fm afc circuits. The varactors are color coded into characteristic groups. Be sure to replace a defective varactor with another from the same color group. The local oscillator varactor is a specially selected varactor. The oscillator varactor is selected for best correlation between capacitance and reverse bias voltage. This gives more consistent dial calibration from set to set. The resistors between the tuning voltage input and the varactors are used to isolate the varactors from those in other stages. Notice that in the Philco circuit the coupling between the rf amplifier and the mixer is double tuned. This offers better selectivity than a single tuned circuit. Such coupling is much easier when varactors are used as the tuning element. Variable capacitors and PTM units occupy too much room in such circuits.

I-F AMPLIFIERS

The i-f amplifier is the section of the radio receiver that provides most of the overall system gain and the selectivity. The i-f amplifier in fm radios usually consists of three or four stages in cascade. One stage of a typical bipolar transistor i-f amplifier is shown in Fig. 3-11. This circuit uses an npn transistor in a common-emitter configuration. Resonant transformers, tapped to provide for the low impedance of the transistor, provide input and output coupling. The capacitance of the transistor, or any triode device for that matter, can cause a feedback signal that can result in unwanted oscillation of the stage. This is especially true of a stage that has both the input and output tuned to the same frequency. In such stages it is

rather easy for the transistor to act as a tuned-base tuned-collector oscillator. The 1.1-pF capacitor connected between the output transformer and the transistor base provides degenerative feedback that tends to cancel any positive feedback due to interelement capacitance.

As illustrated in Fig. 3-12, there are several means of providing interstage coupling for solid-state i-f amplifiers. In Fig. 3-12A, you see the standard tapped resonant-transformer used by most car radios. The tap provides a match for the low-impedance transistors, while the entire winding is used to resonate with the capacitor. This allows a higher "Q" and better bandpass characteristics. The quadra-tuned circuit in Fig. 3-12B is popular as the input coupling to a cascade i-f amplifier chain. Such circuits consist of two resonant tanks coupled by a reactance that is mutually included in both tanks. Fig. 3-12C is the newest type of i-f amplifier coupling. This circuit uses piezoelectric ceramic filter elements as the tuned circuit. These crystal filters are available with a wide variety of bandpass and center-frequency characteristics and are also color coded according to the specifications. It is mandatory that replacement be of the same color group as the original unless all similar

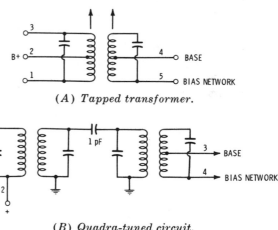

(A) Tapped transformer.

(B) Quadra-tuned circuit.

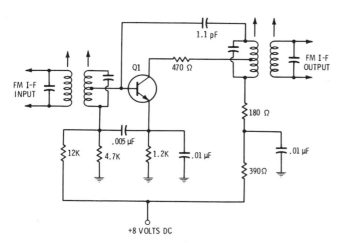

Fig. 3-11. Typical bipolar transistor i-f amplifier.

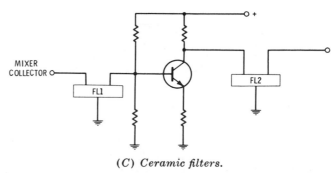

(C) Ceramic filters.

Fig. 3-12. Typical interstage coupling methods used in solid-state i-f amplifiers.

filters in a set are replaced using new filters all within one color code group. In this case, it may be necessary to realign the front end. Ceramic filters are more compact than the wound-coil i-f transformers, and they do not go out of alignment. They fail, to be sure, but they maintain their relative alignment over a wide range of conditions.

Fig. 3-13 is the schematic (Delco) of a composite a-m and fm i-f amplifier. This type of circuit, although a little complex, offers the economy of using a single transistor for both a-m and fm sections. A typical radio might also use the first fm i-f as the a-m rf, the second fm i-f as the a-m converter, and the third fm i-f as the a-m i-f. Some radios, notably those of European or Japanese origin, also use the fourth fm if/limiter stage as a second a-m i-f. The Delco circuit of Fig. 3-13 has an interesting feature. Notice that the fm transformer feeds the emitter of the transistor, while the a-m input transformer feeds the base. This stage is common emitter on a-m and common base on fm. The primaries of T2 and T4 i-f transformers are series connected. This is permitted because of the wide separation in the relative inductance values. The fm i-f primary (T2) is a very low-inductance coil. The a-m i-f primary has relatively high inductance. On fm, the signal will be coupled through T2 and then be bypassed to ground around T4 by a 470-pF capacitor. On a-m, the i-f signal is allowed to pass through the T2 primary because of its low inductance (the impedance offered to the a-m i-f signal by the fm coil is considered negligible) and be coupled through T4.

Fig. 3-14 is a type of composite i-f amplifier used by Philips of Canada in the radios made for Chrys-

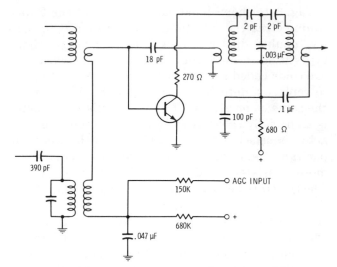

Fig. 3-14. A Philips composite a-m and fm i-f amplifier stage.

ler. In this arrangement both a-m and fm i-f amplifiers are in the common-emitter configuration.

The integrated circuit (IC) has been successfully used in car radio fm i-f amplifiers for several years. One of the earliest practical IC stages is the

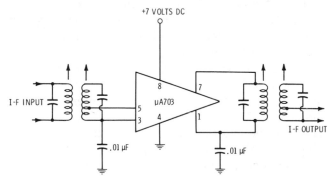

Fig. 3-15. Integrated-circuit (µA703) fm i-f amplifier.

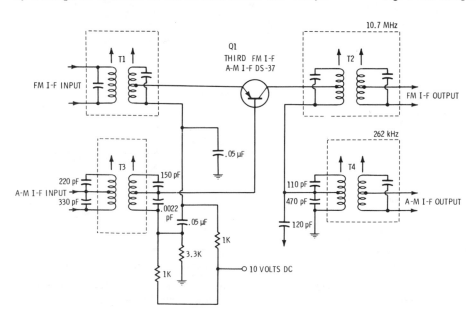

Fig. 3-13. Composite a-m and fm i-f amplifier stage.

circuit shown in Fig. 3-15. This circuit uses a well-known IC, the Type µA703, as the active element. This type IC has been used in many fm and fm stereo receivers of both automotive and home designs. The µA703 is not, however, the only IC to see extensive service as an fm i-f amplifier. Many designs now feature ICs made by many semiconductor manufacturers.

LIMITERS

The limiter stage is one of the reasons for the freedom from noise enjoyed by fm listeners. In frequency modulation, the transmitter carrier frequency is varied by the audio modulation. In amplitude modulation it is the carrier intensity, or amplitude, that is varied while the carrier frequency remains constant. It is fortunate that most of the static interference to radio reception tends to create unwanted amplitude variations. If you can clip off these spurious amplitude variations without losing the audio, you can eliminate most noise interference. The limiter stage is designed to accomplish this function. The limiter is essentially an amplifier with not enough gain for the amplitude of its input signal. The limiter will, therefore, clip the peaks of the signal and eliminate the noise. Since frequency variations contain the audio information sought by the detector, the limiter will have no effect on the recovered program material. In an a-m radio, however, a limiter stage will severely distort the recovered audio.

DETECTORS

Before the high fidelity of fm can be enjoyed, the signal must be demodulated. There are several types of detector circuits used in car radios for demodulation. One of the most common forms of detector is the almost traditional Foster-Seeley discriminator illustrated in Fig. 3-16. The fm detection in a discriminator depends upon the phase relationship between the signal voltages in each half of the tuned secondary and the tuned primary. When tuned to exactly 10.7 MHz with a 10.7-MHz unmodulated signal present at the input, the signals fed to the two diodes are exactly 90° out of phase with each other and 45° out of phase with the primary signal. These voltages are equal but of opposite polarity. This causes the rectified output from the two diodes to cancel—resulting in a zero dc output voltage. When the signal is frequency modulated, however, the phase relationships change in step with the modulation so that the out-

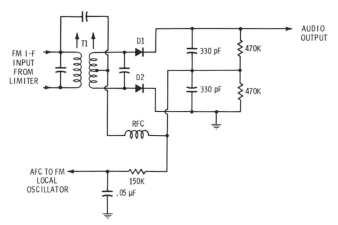

Fig. 3-16. A common fm discriminator.

puts will no longer cancel. The result is a dc level changing at the frequency of the audio modulating rate. The voltage on the afc line will be exactly zero when the incoming signal is tuned to the exact center frequency.

The chief difference between the ratio detector of Fig. 3-17 and a discriminator circuit is the polarity of the diodes. In a discriminator, the diode output voltages tend to buck each other. In a ratio detector circuit, however, they tend to add. The relative contribution of the two diodes is 2:1 when the input signal is unmodulated. As the audio modulation varies the input signal, the relative contribution of each diode changes in step with the audio. The signal output is relative to the ratio of the diode outputs. One feature of ratio detector is the a-m suppression capacitor connected across the two diode circuits. This capacitor will reduce spurious noises to a point where a limiter stage is

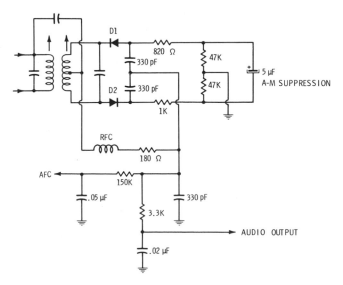

Fig. 3-17. Typical fm ratio detector.

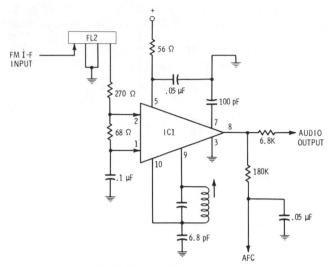

Fig. 3-18. Bendix IC detector circuit.

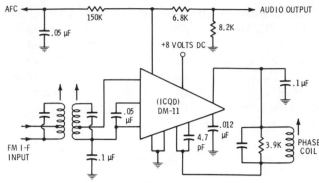

Fig. 3-20. External circuitry of a
Delco ICQD stage.

not needed. In fact, many fm sets using the ratio detector do not have a limiter stage.

Integrated circuits are frequently used in fm detection. There are a number of different ICs available for this service. There are ICs with independent internal diodes that can be connected either as a discriminator or as a ratio detector. Some other types of IC fm detectors are of the quadrature type. Fig. 3-18 is an IC detector circuit used by Bendix. The input is taken directly from the output terminals of a ceramic i-f filter. The output is taken from pin 8 and is then fed to the audio amplifier section.

A Delco IC quadrature detector (ICQD) block diagram is shown in Fig. 3-19. In this circuit the fm i-f signal is first processed by three internal, high gain, wideband limiter/amplifier stages. The output from the third stage is a limited square wave. At this point the signal is split into two components. One is fed directly to the detector. The other is phase shifted 90° by an external LC network. The phase-shifted signal is then fed to

the detector. The actual detector circuit is of the gated-coincidence type. When the input signal is unmodulated and is the frequency that will shift exactly 90° in the LC network, the detector output will be zero. When the signal is modulated, however, the output will be a series of pulses of varying width and period that can be integrated into an audio signal.

Fig. 3-20 shows the external components that must be used with the Delco ICQD. The input transformer is a standard fm i-f type. The other tuned circuit, however, is a simple LC tank circuit designated as the *phase coil*. It is critical that this phase coil be precisely aligned to produce a 90° phase shift at 10.7 MHz. Misalignment of the coil can cause an increased distortion level, decreased output, and excessive noise levels. The IC has provisions for an afc control signal. The phase coil is the chief identifying factor in determining whether an IC is a quadrature detector; the fact that an IC is used in the detector does not determine this. If you see the familiar discriminator or ratio detector transformer being used in conjunction with an IC, it is not a quadrature detector. In these cases, normal fm alignment techniques will suffice.

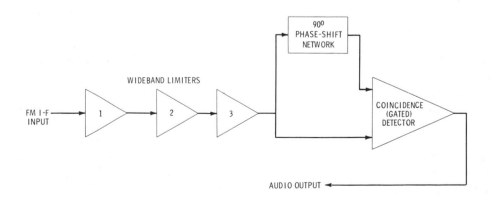

Fig. 3-19. Block diagram of a Delco
IC quadrature detector.

Chapter 4

Multiplex Section

The advent of fm stereo broadcasting opened a new electronic entertainment medium for those who enjoy good sound. Not to be outdone by makers of home fm receivers, the auto radio suppliers have jumped into the fm stereo market with both feet. In fact, it is now difficult, if not impossible, to obtain a factory original monaural fm car radio. This chapter deals with the stereo signal from the detector output to the audio amplifier input and the particular types of fm stereo circuits used in processing the signal.

One of the initial requirements for fm stereo is that it must be compatible with existing monaural fm receivers. In order to meet this requirement, it is necessary to *multiplex* an encoded version of the stereo information onto the regular fm carrier in such a way that it can be decoded in a stereo receiver and yet does not interfere with monaural reception. Figs. 4-1 and 4-2 show how this is accomplished. Both left and right channel audio are combined into a monaural signal called the "L+R." The spectrum chart of Fig. 4-1 shows how this signal appears in relation to the rest of the audio spectrum. The L+R signal allows a monaural receiver to offer the listener both channels without any loss other than stereo separation.

The encoded stereo information is centered about 38 kHz. This signal is called the "L−R." The "minus R" designation simply means that the two channels are combined, with the right channel signal being phase shifted 180°. An amplifier stage can accomplish this phase reversal, so that the rigors of designing a wideband audio phase-shift network are avoided. The L−R output is fed to a balanced modulator. The output signal from the balanced modulator is a double-sideband suppressed carrier (dsbsc) form of amplitude modulation. In a properly working system, the 38-kHz subcarrier is suppressed so that only the L−R sidebands created by the modulation process remain. Since an fm broadcast station is allowed to transmit audio frequencies up to 15 kHz, the sideband will occupy the spectrum around 38 kHz—plus and minus 15 kHz or 23 to 53 kHz. The dsbsc output from the balanced modulator, now called the composite signal, is fed to an fm modulator along with the L+R monaural signal. A third signal is also sent to the fm modulator. It is a pilot signal at one-half the frequency of the 38-kHz subcarrier (19 kHz). The pilot is needed at the receiver stereo decoder to reconstruct the subcarrier with precisely the same frequency and phase that it had during the modulation process.

BLOCK DIAGRAM

Fig. 4-3 is the block diagram of a typical multiplex section. This circuitry is positioned in the radio between the audio output of the fm detector and the inputs of the two audio amplifier chains needed for proper rendition of the stereo signal.

The first stage of the decoder encountered by the composite signals is the preamplifier/signal splitter. Besides building up the amplitude of part of the signal, this stage also separates the various components (Fig. 4-1) and sends them on to their proper places.

The 19-kHz pilot signal is usually taken from the collector of the splitter amplifier transistor via a resonant tuned transformer or simple tank circuit. It is then amplified further before being used to regenerate the suppressed 38-kHz subcarrier.

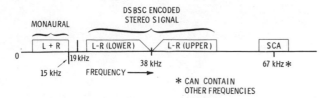

Fig. 4-1. Stereo (fm) composite signal spectrum chart.

Any one of several possible regeneration methods may be found in a specific car radio design. The 38-kHz signal is then fed to RC-diode decoder matrix circuitry.

The remainder of the composite signal will contain L+R, L−R, 19 kHz, and possibly 67-kHz SCA information. The SCA is another subcarrier system used to provide background music in such places as stores and offices. In the stereo receiver, we are only interested in the L+R and L−R signals. In order to purify the splitter output, it is necessary to include resonant traps that will either block or shunt to ground any SCA (67 kHz) or 19-kHz signal that reaches the composite side of the splitter amplifier.

A composite amplifier may follow the traps. In some sets this amplifier is used for both signal delay and composite amplification. In any event, not all fm stereo car radios include a composite amplifier. The L+R and L−R output from the composite amplifier is fed to the decoder, where it is combined with the regenerated 38-kHz subcarrier. The new subcarrier must be locked to the pilot signal so that phase and frequency differences between it and the original subcarrier are minimized. The recovered left- and right-channel audio signals are

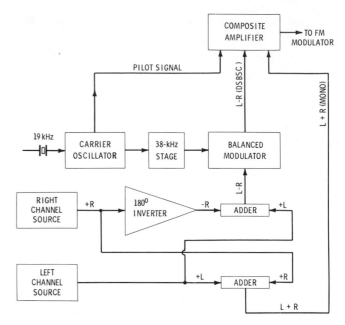

Fig. 4-2. Block diagram of stereo generator/transmitter.

generally fed to the preamplifier stages of the audio sections via filters that remove any residual 38-kHz subcarrier signal. Most stereo receivers isolate the decoder from the rest of the radio by placing emitter-follower buffer amplifiers at the decoder output. These buffers may also contain the 75 microsecond de-emphasis network needed to restore the frequency response balance of the audio signals.

Most fm stereo receivers incorporate a beacon lamp to indicate when the set is tuned to a stereo station. Most beacons are triggered by the presence of either the 19- or 38-kHz signals. Later in

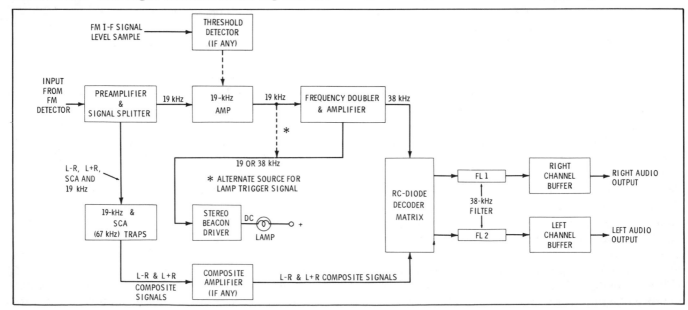

Fig. 4-3. Block diagram of a multiplex section for a car radio.

this chapter we will take a look at some of the many circuits used to control the beacon lamp.

INPUT STAGE

Fig. 4-4 is a sophisticated type of preamplifier stage. This type of circuit combines both the pre-amplifier and splitter functions. For best stereo reception it is necessary to split the various components of the composite signal prior to any further processing. In this circuit the 19-kHz pilot signal is taken from the collector of the splitter transistor by a tuned transformer. The collector output from the splitter is designed in such a way that it will reject all components of the composite signal except the pilot. The L+R and L−R signals are taken from the emitter of the splitter transistor. In this particular design there is a parallel-resonant SCA trap in series with the signal path and a series-resonant 19-kHz trap across the signal path. The series-resonant 19-kHz trap will offer a low impedance to the 19-kHz signal and a high impedance to all other frequencies. Because of this, it will shunt only the pilot signal to ground while allowing the L+R and L−R signals to pass.

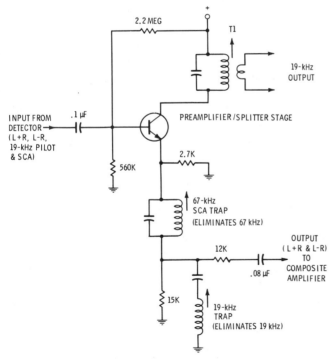

Fig. 4-4. Sophisticated preamplifier stage.

COMPOSITE AMPLIFIER

A simple composite (buffer) amplifier is illustrated in Fig. 4-5. This circuit is a Delco design.

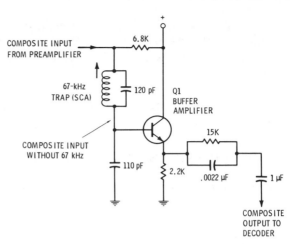

Fig. 4-5. Simple composite (buffer) amplifier.

It is an emitter follower with a 67-kHz parallel-resonant trap in series with the base input lead. This trap is adjusted using a 67-kHz signal from either an fm stereo generator or an audio oscillator. An oscilloscope or ac vtvm is used to monitor the signal level at the emitter of the preamplifier transistor. Adjust the slug of the coil so that minimum 67-kHz signal gets through the trap. (Parallel-resonant traps block their resonant frequency.)

PILOT AMPLIFIER

Fig. 4-6 shows a typical 19-kHz pilot amplifier. This common-emitter stage resembles an i-f amplifier. Indeed, except for the difference in frequency requirements, it might easily serve as an i-f amplifier. This type of amplifier is positioned between the 19-kHz splitter output and the 38-kHz circuitry. The Bendix circuit chosen for Fig. 4-6 includes a gating input. This input is driven by a threshold detector in the fm limiter circuit. Stereo reception can be noisy and unpleasant when the broadcast station signal is too weak. The threshold detector/gated pilot amplifier system keeps the

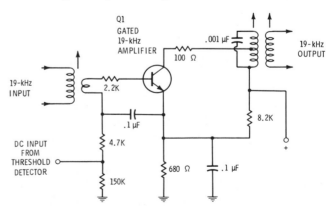

Fig. 4-6. Typical 19-kHz pilot amplifier.

stereo circuitry turned off unless a certain minimum signal strength is available. Zero dc voltage on the base and a slight positive voltage on the emitter keeps Q1 reverse biased. The threshold detector triggers a positive voltage sufficient to forward-bias Q1, so that it can pass the 19-kHz pilot signal.

OBTAINING THE 38-kHz SIGNAL

The decoder action requires a signal which is twice the frequency of the pilot signal. This 38-kHz signal also must be in phase with the pilot signal. The standard is that both signals must cross the zero axis in a positive-going direction at the same instant.

Locked Oscillator

There are two basic methods for regenerating the subcarrier. One is the locked oscillator technique used by Delco for several years, and the other is the frequency multiplier technique used by numerous other manufacturers. An example of the locked oscillator is shown in Fig. 4-7. The basic configuration is called the Hartley oscillator cir-

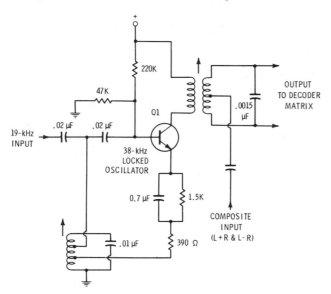

Fig. 4-7. A 38-kHz locked oscillator.

cuit. In this type of circuit the feedback is supplied by a tapped coil functioning as an inductive voltage divider. The 19-kHz pilot signal controls the frequency and phase of the locked oscillator output. The pilot signal is fed to both the base of the oscillator transistor and to a second tap on the oscillator coil. Output from the oscillator is coupled through a transformer in the collector. The primary of this transformer is untuned to prevent

the oscillator from breaking lock because of the influence of a second tuned circuit.

An oscilloscope is the best method for adjusting the locked oscillator coil. Connect the vertical input of the oscilloscope to the collector of the 19-kHz amplifier. Similarly, connect the 38-kHz output transformer secondary to the horizontal input of the oscilloscope. With the sweep selector set to "external," we should see a 1:2 Lissajous pattern. If the oscillator is not locked to the pilot signal, this pattern will rotate. The speed of rotation will be determined by the amount of frequency error. Adjust the slug of the oscillator coil until the pattern locks. Try tuning the radio on and off several stereo stations in order to determine whether or not the adjustment is correct. There is a narrow range over which the oscillator will lock. If the oscillator slug is set too close to an edge of that range, the circuit may not lock properly every time. It is necessary to find a setting that will allow a proper lock on all acceptable stations every time.

Frequency Doubler

Fig. 4-8 illustrates what has become the most common method for regenerating the subcarrier. This is the frequency doubler stage. In this stage the 19-kHz amplifier output transformer has a center-tapped (full-wave) secondary winding. The center tap is grounded while the winding extremities feed diode rectifiers. These diodes convert the 19-kHz signal into a series of half-wave pulses. Because this type of rectifier operates on both halves of the input waveform, the repetition rate of these pulses is 38 kHz. The 38-kHz output of the doubler is fed to a 38-kHz amplifier. This stage has the dual function of building up the amplitude of the pulses and converting them back into sine waves. This is necessary because the decoder needs good, clean sine waves in order to offer maximum stereo separation. The conversion of pulses to sine waves occurs because of the flywheel effect of the tuned transformer in the amplifier output circuit. In this type of stage, adjustments can be made with either an oscilloscope or an ac vtvm. All that is necessary to align the stage is to peak the various tuned transformers.

DECODER NETWORK

A typical stereo decoder network is shown in Fig. 4-9. This is a diode-resistor type of circuit. The 38-kHz subcarrier is used to switch the diodes into and out of conduction. The input transformer

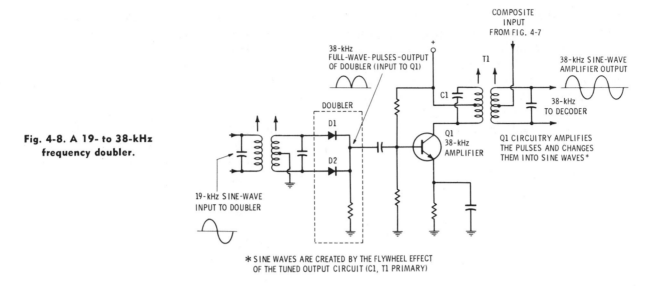

Fig. 4-8. A 19- to 38-kHz frequency doubler.

is a full wave affair with the L+R and L−R composite information fed to the center tap. The 38-kHz subcarrier is fed to the primary of the transformer. Recovered right- and left-channel audio is taken from the output resistor terminals and is fed, through 38-kHz filters, to buffer amplifiers.

stalling a stereo adapter in some monaural radios, it might be necessary to remove the existing de-emphasis network in the fm detector circuit. It seems that the high frequency de-emphasis curve attenuates the 19-kHz pilot signal to a point where it cannot trigger the stereo adapter.

Fig. 4-9. Typical stereo decoder network.

BUFFER AMPLIFIERS

A pair of buffer amplifiers from a Delco stereo adapter are the subject of Fig. 4-10. These stages are emitter followers used to isolate the decoder from the remaining audio circuitry. In most automotive stereo sets, these buffers are also used to provide the 75 microsecond de-emphasis. When in-

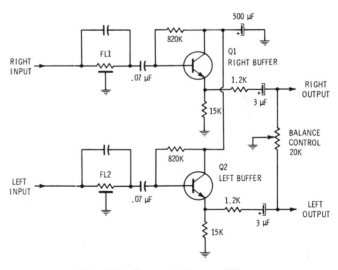

Fig. 4-10. Stereo buffer amplifiers.

BEACON LAMPS

Although a stereo program has a distinctly different effect than a traditional monaural program, it is still considered desirable to include a beacon lamp to let the listener know when he is tuned to an fm stereo station. These beacon lamps operate by detecting the presence of either the pilot (19 kHz) or the subcarrier (38 kHz). One of the simplest stereo beacon circuits is shown in Fig. 4-11. This particular circuit is common among Japanese

car radio and radio/tape player combination designs. In this type of circuit the 38-kHz amplifier (Q1) is biased to cut off when the set is not tuned to a stereo station. The pulses generated by the frequency doubler, however, will forward-bias the 38-kHz amplifier transistor. When this occurs, Q1 will begin to draw collector current. The collector current will cause a voltage drop across R1. This

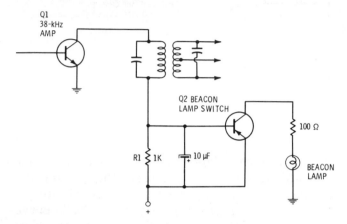

Fig. 4-11. Simple stereo beacon circuit.

voltage drop is used to forward-bias the pnp transistor used as a beacon lamp switch. When this occurs, Q2 conducts, drawing current through the lamp. To stabilize the dc voltage drop across R1, many circuits will parallel R1 with a capacitor to bypass the 38-kHz signal. This prevents all but the strongest noise pulses from causing lamp flicker. A related circuit used by Bendix in their stereo models produced for Ford is shown in Fig. 4-12.

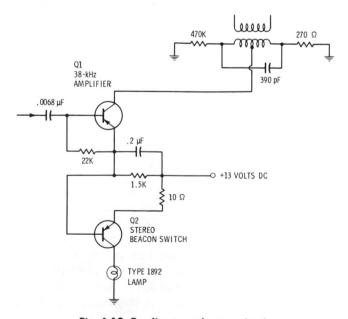

Fig. 4-12. Bendix stereo beacon circuit.

Early Delco underdash stereo adapters used a more complex lamp circuit as shown in Fig. 4-13. In this circuit the 19-kHz information is taken from the pilot amplifier and is applied to the lamp pre-amplifier transistor. This signal is then amplified and passed to the lamp circuit. The lamp amplifier transistor Q2 is biased to a point just below cut-off. The amplified 19-kHz signal applied to the base of Q2 is sufficient to cause a forward-bias condition. When this occurs, the transistor will begin to conduct, and a voltage drop will be created across the emitter resistor. This voltage is then used to forward-bias the lamp relay control transistor Q3. A relay coil is used as the emitter load of Q3. When Q3 begins to conduct, its emitter current energizes the relay. A disadvantage to this early circuit was that variations in signal strength could cause the relay to turn on and off. The resultant "clickety-clack" of the relay armature was quite annoying. In later versions of the stereo adapter, Delco substituted the solid-state relay of Fig. 4-14.

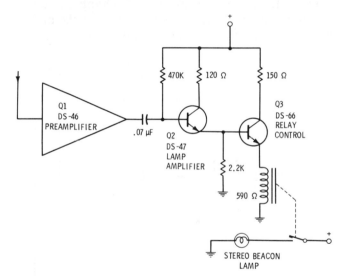

Fig. 4-13. Delco relay-operated stereo beacon circuit.

Fig. 4-14 is a more silent method of accomplishing beacon turn on. In this circuit a sample of the 38-kHz subcarrier is applied to a half-wave voltage doubler circuit. The output from this doubler is a negative dc voltage. It is applied to the base of the lamp preamplifier transistor Q1. Applying a negative voltage to the base of an npn transistor will cause it to cut off. When Q1 is cut off, no collector current can flow. This means that due to a decreased voltage drop across the collector load resistor (R2), the collector voltage will go up. In this direct-coupled circuit such an increase in voltage will be sufficient to forward-bias npn transistor Q2. When Q2 begins to conduct because of

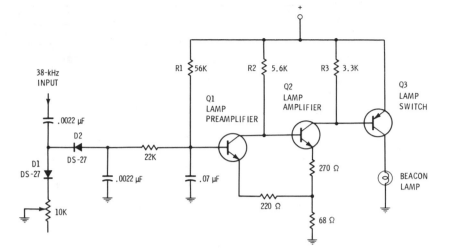

Fig. 4-14. Delco solid-state stereo beacon circuit.

the applied forward bias, its collector voltage will drop. Since the collector of Q2 is direct coupled to the base of Q3 (the pnp lamp switch transistor) it causes the lamp switch to turn on. When the radio is tuned to a nonstereo station or to no station at all, the negative voltage at the output of the voltage doubler ceases to exist. This will cause Q1 to saturate, cutting off the forward-bias to Q2. At this point, the collector voltage of Q2 rises to a point where Q3 turns off. In some models there is a variable resistor in the voltage doubler to control the lamp sensitivity.

IC DECODERS

Several years ago, Motorola Semiconductor Products developed an integrated-circuit stereo decoder. This decoder is housed in a fourteen-lead dual inline package made of plastic. Its dimensions

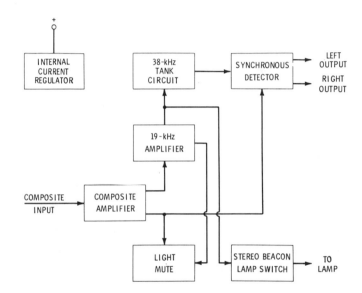

Fig. 4-15. Motorola IC decoder (MC1304) block diagram.

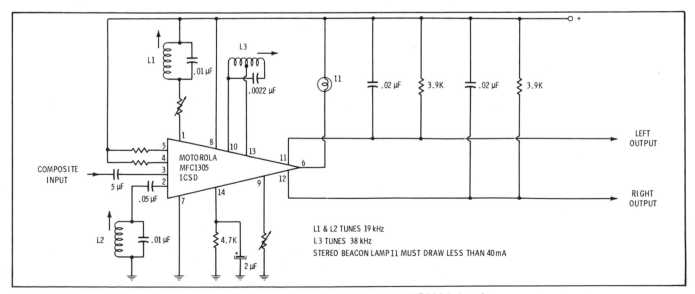

L1 & L2 TUNES 19 kHz
L3 TUNES 38 kHz
STEREO BEACON LAMP I1 MUST DRAW LESS THAN 40 mA

Fig. 4-16. External circuitry for Motorola MC1304 decoder.

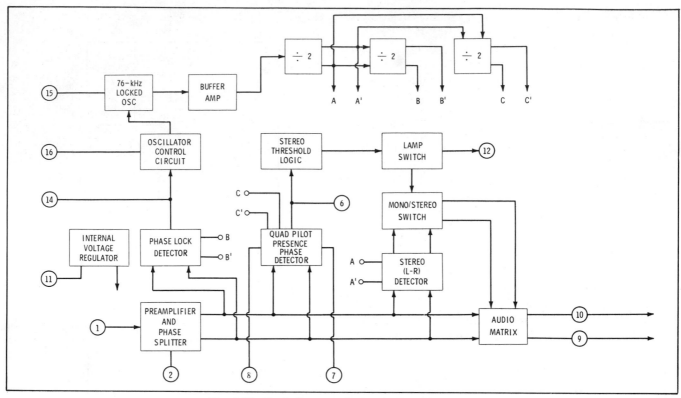

Fig. 4-17. Block diagram of a Bendix digital decoder.

are approximately three-tenths of an inch wide by seven-eighths of an inch long. A partial block diagram of what is inside this IC is shown in Fig. 4-15. Notice that it contains all of the essential circuitry needed for stereo decoding. The decoder itself is a synchronous type that is generally more effective than the simpler diode-resistor type. This IC also includes provisions for both muting and for

a stereo beacon. A typical external circuit using the Motorola MC1304/1305 series IC is shown in Fig. 4-16. In this particular circuit, the mute function is permanently biased. Other circuits permit the user to determine whether or not muting is needed. The lamp is connected directly to the beacon terminal (pin 6) on the IC. In some other circuits, the lamp terminal is connected to the base of a pnp lamp-

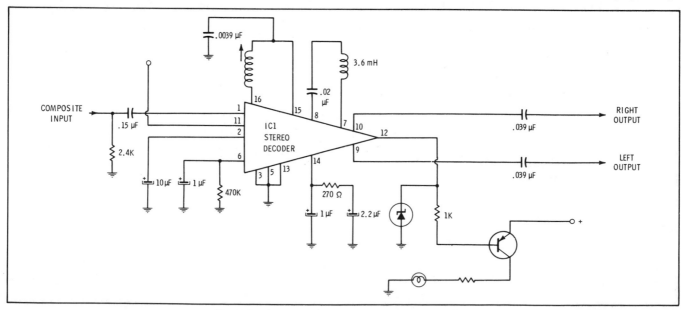

Fig. 4-18. External circuitry for the Bendix decoder.

switching transistor. This allows the use of higher current lamps, while simultaneously reducing internal heating of the IC. These ICs, or closely related cousins in the same line, are widely used by several car radio manufacturers. Motorola Automotive Products uses it in many of their car radio models. Delco uses ICs of the same family, under the type numbers DM-14 and DM-24, in their most recent car stereo radios. Even Becker *AutoRadio* of Germany uses the MC1304 IC in the *Europa MU* (stereo) radios made for Mercedes-Benz.

A newer type of IC stereo decoder used by Bendix is shown in Figs. 4-17 and 4-18. It is called the digital decoder and RCA offers a similar decoder in their semiconductor catalog. The interesting fea-

ture of this decoder is the phase-locked oscillator. This stage operates at a frequency that is twice the subcarrier frequency (2 × 38 kHz = 76 kHz). The output from this oscillator is fed to a series of stages that divide the 76 kHz down to first 38 kHz and then 19 kHz. The frequency of the oscillator is the only adjustment needed in this circuit. The adjustment does not have to be especially accurate because of the voltage controlled oscillator (vco) design. If the adjustment is even close, the phase lock detector and the oscillator control circuit will bring the output of the oscillator to the exact frequency. This circuit is alleged to offer superior performance over earlier designs.

Chapter 5

Power-Supply Section

Except for older American sets and some foreign sets, the universal power requirement for automotive electronic equipment is a 12-volt dc source. Although some radios will operate from either positive or negative ground, the standard American system for well over a decade is negative ground. Some foreign cars, however, retain the use of positive grounding.

Fig. 5-1 shows a partial schematic of the standard automotive electrical system. A lead-acid storage battery is used to supply power. The battery is continuously recharged by either a dc generator or an alternator (rectified ac) and fed through a voltage regulator. Most cars feed power to the radio or tape player from the "switched" side of the ignition switch. Some autos, again mostly foreign types, have only one hot position on the ignition switch. The majority of American cars, however, have two positions that supply power to the accessories. One of these is the normal *on* position. The other is called the *accessory* position. In the latter position all systems will operate except the ignition and sometimes the lights. The purpose of this arrangement is to allow the radio to be played while the car is parked. It is mandatory that the engine be running whenever the switch is left in the "on" position. This is necessary in order to prevent damage to the breaker points, ignition coil, and any electrical fuel pumps that may be in use. In older installations and most modern after-market installations, the radio has its own in-line fuse holder. In these designs, the power wire from the radio is often connected to a long threaded stud on the back of the ignition switch. Most modern cars, however, make use of a master fuse box. Power to the individual systems is distributed from the fuse box.

There are two basic types of switching used in automotive electronic equipment. One of these, shown in Fig. 5-2A, utilizes a simple spst (single-pole, single-throw) switch mounted on the back of the volume control. Another widely used system (Fig. 5-2B) makes use of a dpst (double-pole, single-throw) switch. In the latter arrangement, one section is used to supply power to the radio circuits, while the other supplies power to the pilot lamp.

BASIC CIRCUITS

Fig. 5-3 illustrates the typical power supply used in a wide variety of car radios. The positive side of this supply is connected to the radio on-off switch. Notice that the supply voltage input is marked 14 volts. Most modern automotive electrical systems are rated at 12 volts. This is only a nominal value. Most auto makers specify some actual value between 13.2 and 14.4 volts dc. It is important that this figure be remembered when replacing parts that have a maximum voltage rating. If C1 were replaced with a 500-μF capacitor rated at 12 volts, the new capacitor would probably become shorted. Resistors R1 and R2 serve to reduce the voltage to the levels required by the various stages in the radio. The audio power amplifiers are powered directly from the output side of the choke (L1).

The purpose of choke L1 is to offer opposition to noise pulses from the ignition system and other electrical devices. It has a relatively high imped-

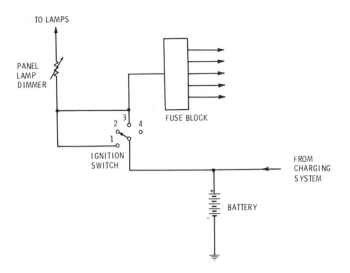

Fig. 5-1. Partial schematic of the standard automotive electrical system.

ance but a low dc resistance. These noise chokes are frequently made with a cylindrical ferrite core not unlike the loopstick antenna used in portable radios. Most often, however, the noise choke will be of the channel mounting type that has a laminated iron core. The value will be somewhere near the one henry range.

In Fig. 5-3, the 200-pF spark plate capacitor serves to attenuate incoming noise pulses. Fig. 5-4 offers a detailed view of a typical spark plate capacitor construction. This style of capacitor is made of two pieces of copper foil sandwiched over a *fishpaper* dielectric. The value is nominal, since it will change somewhat as the fishpaper soaks up moisture. The physical dimensions of the spark plate will be less than two inches square. Do not replace a spark plate with another type of capacitor of similar value. These capacitors will gener-

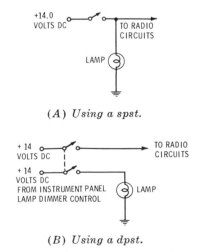

(A) Using a spst.

(B) Using a dpst.

Fig. 5-2. Typical power switching circuits for the car radio.

ally be located within an inch of the point where the power line enters the radio. One side will be sweat-soldered to the radio chassis. The power lead is soldered to the hot side. Do not use the spark plate as the point to connect power unless it has been confirmed as the power lead. Other spark plates may be used at the "hot" side of the speaker leads. An incorrect choice can easily burn up the output choke.

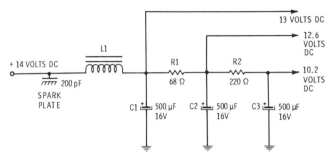

Fig. 5-3. Standard power supply for a car radio.

Besides suppressing externally generated noise pulses, the filter capacitors must also perform other functions. One of these is to decouple the signal voltages entering the power system from the various radio stages. Since all stages are fed from a common power-supply line, it is easy for signal

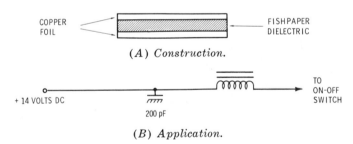

(A) Construction.

(B) Application.

Fig. 5-4. Typical spark plate.

voltages to stray from one stage to another via the supply line. The filter capacitors prevent this by passing the ac signal voltages to ground while maintaining the dc at its prescribed level. Should one of these capacitors become open, positive feedback can occur. This will cause the radio to oscillate. The low-impedance path offered to ac signal voltages by the filter capacitors is also useful as the ground return for the signals in the various stages. This results in a higher stage gain than would otherwise be possible. Even if the decoupling function could be avoided by the use of separate power supplies for each stage (which is totally impractical), the filter capacitors would still be necessary to provide the low-impedance ac ground return path.

VOLTAGE REGULATION

Modern car radios, especially fm car radios, require a fairly tight degree of voltage regulation. Unfortunately, the average automotive voltage regulator does not do much regulating from the radio designer's point of view. A typical automotive electrical system will vary from 12 to almost 15 volts dc as the car accelerates from zero to sixty miles per hour. This variation will cause an fm car radio to change frequency over a range that covers several fm channels. To eliminate this problem, radio designers incorporate an internal voltage regulator in all fm car radios. The most common form of voltage regulator is the zener diode. When used properly, this type of diode will maintain a relatively constant voltage drop across its terminals. An example of such a voltage regulator is shown in Fig. 5-5A. This particular circuit is from a Delco radio by General Motors. The DS-149 zener diode maintains a constant 8-volt level over a wide range of input voltages. It is not uncommon to find a zener regulating the 8-volt line to within a fraction of a volt, while the input voltage varies from 10 to 16 volts. This 8-volt value is very common in car radio circuits. The voltage rating is strictly nominal; the actual voltage will be between approximately 7.5 and 8.5 volts. This voltage may easily be different even in different examples of the same model. The voltage may also vary with temperature. The important thing is that the zener voltage remain relatively constant. Some of the more recent radios are using two terminals of a transistor as the zener diode. All pn semiconductor junctions exhibit a zener effect. In the example

shown in Fig. 5-5B, Motorola has used the base and emitter terminals of an npn transistor as the zener regulator. This technique has become more and more widely used.

For several years some car radio manufacturers have been using transistor series regulator circuits to keep the B+ line at a constant value. One such regulator, used by Philco in the 1972 Ford fm stereo radios, is illustrated in Fig. 5-6. This circuit also functions as the am/fm bandswitch. A voltage divider made of resistors R1 and R2 provides the a-m B+ voltage. When the bandswitch (S1) is open, the B+ is applied to the a-m sections of the radio. When S1 is closed, the a-m B+ line is shorted to common. This switch also closes the ground connection of the zener-regulated base circuit for Q1. The fm B+ appears at the collector of Q1 and is dependent upon the rating of the zener.

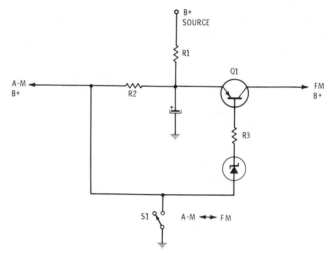

Fig. 5-6. Philco transistor series-regulator circuit.

A similar circuit is shown in Fig. 5-7. This particular regulated power supply is used in some of the fm stereo radios made for Chrysler by Philips Ltd. of Canada. In this circuit a transistor series regulator is used to feed a resistive voltage-divider network. The audio stages of the radio are fed from the unregulated 13.2-volt tap. Stages prior to the audio are fed from one of the regulated tops. The final tap, the 6.2-volt dc source, is zener regulated.

The newer Bendix fm radios use still another type of voltage regulator circuit. This circuit, shown in Fig. 5-8, combines zener, series, and shunt regulation methods. One interesting feature of this supply is the circuitry of transistor Q1. Should the supply voltage from the automobile battery fall below the range of voltages that can be tolerated by the radio circuitry, Q1 will cut the set

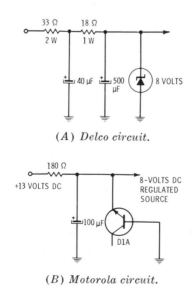

(A) Delco circuit.

(B) Motorola circuit.

Fig. 5-5. Simple voltage regulators for a car radio.

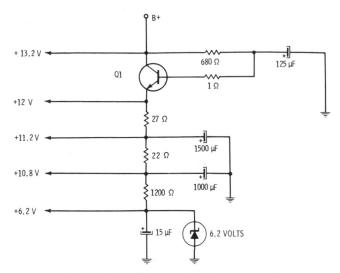

Fig. 5-7. A Philips regulated power supply for an fm stereo.

off by reverse-biasing the regulator transistors Q2 and Q3. When the supply voltage is in excess of the nominal 8-volt rating of the zener, the current passing through the zener keeps Q1 in a forward-biased state. When the supply voltage drops below the zener breakover voltage, no current can flow and Q1 is thus cut off. This allows the collector voltage of Q1 to rise high enough to reverse-bias and cut off Q2. The unregulated line is used to power the audio amplifier output stage. The 12.5-volt regulated line is used to power the fm stages and the operational amplifier used in the audio preamp stages.

GROUNDING

A reversed car-battery polarity can fool almost any accessory or circuit in the vehicle except one that has transistors or other solid-state electronic components. Since most radios are negative ground designs, it is imperative that they be used only in vehicles that are also negative grounded. The results of improper polarity operation can be disastrous for the radio. The usual result is that the audio power-amplifier transistor is destroyed. The other stages are also affected but are rarely destroyed. This is due to the relatively large amount of resistance in series with the power source and the transistors. The power amplifier, however, is usually operated directly from the output of the noise choke. There is little resistance in series with this transistor, so current can flow in amounts that appear almost unimpeded as far as the transistor is concerned. A simple precaution to guard against improper polarity is shown in Fig. 5-9A. A simple rectifier diode in series with the power or "hot" lead (the lead that brings the voltage from the car battery to the radio) will cause the radio to cut off when the battery polarity is reversed. Although this cut off of the radio is undesirable, it is better than the destruction of an expensive power transistor. The voltage drop across this diode in the forward direction will be insignificant enough so that it will not adversely affect operation of the radio.

Transient voltage spikes are frequently the cause of repeated failure in solid-state car radios. Almost any unsuppressed inductive device will generate a transient spike when it is turned off. Should the radio be operating when this occurs, there is a strong possibility of damage to some of the transistors. Some manufacturers use the circuit of Fig. 5-9B to prevent such damage. The diode is a zener regulator type with a voltage rating in excess of the normal range of input voltages for which the equipment is designed. A typical rating for a zener used to protect automotive electronic equipment is 18 or 20 volts. The transients that

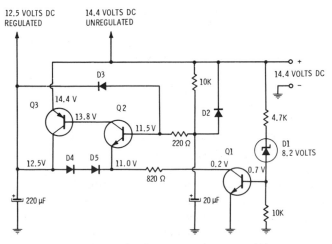

Fig. 5-8. Bendix electronic voltage regulator.

(A) Guards radio against improper battery polarity.

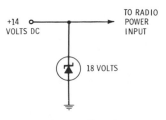

(B) Prevents transient spikes from entering radio.

Fig. 5-9. Diode protection circuits.

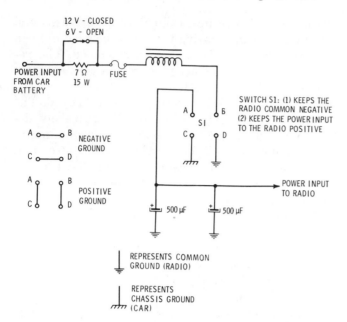

Fig. 5-10. Voltage and polarity switching power supply.

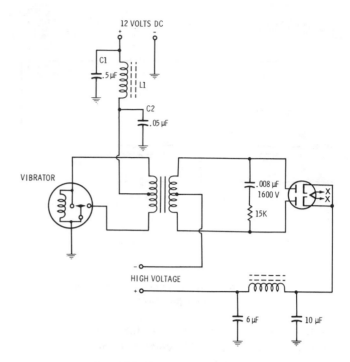

Fig. 5-11. Vibrator power supply.

can destroy the transistors will be of considerably higher voltage. As a result of the zener action, transient peaks will be clipped to a level that will not harm the radio circuitry.

Some after-market car radios will operate in both positive and negative ground automobiles. Since these are solid-state radios, some means for reversing the polarity is needed. Fig. 5-10 illustrates how polarity reversal can be accomplished. A switch or reversing plug is used to make the proper connections. When the radio is used on positive ground cars, the power lead from the car battery is connected to the radio common, while the car chassis (negative) is connected to the power input to the radio. When used on negative ground cars, the power input from the car battery is connected to the power input to the radio, and the radio common is connected to the chassis ground of the car. Most American radios use a seven-pin miniature tube socket and a shorting plug for this polarity reversal.

LOW VOLTAGE TO HIGH VOLTAGE

Before the days of low anode voltage vacuum tubes and all transistor designs, it was necessary to use a car radio power supply that could take the low-voltage dc from the battery and convert it to high-voltage dc needed by the tubes. This requires, of course, a step-up transformer. Since dc will not pass through a transformer, some means was needed to cause the dc to set up a varying magnetic field in the power-transformer primary circuit.

Only a changing magnetic field will allow transformer action. The electromechanical vibrator shown in Fig. 5-11 performs this function. It is essentially an spdt switch driven by a buzzer-like mechanism. The primary side of the power transformer is center tapped. The low-voltage supply is fed to this tap. The vibrator switch contacts alternately ground first one side of the primary, then the other. This causes the changing current flow required to operate the transformer. The switching spikes (transients) caused by vibrator action can cause several problems. One is noise interference with radio reception. To suppress these transients, a ferrite core choke (L1) and two bypass capacitors (C1 and C2) are connected to the power line. Component-damaging spikes from the high-voltage side of the power transformer are suppressed by the buffer capacitor and resistor connected across the secondary winding. Previously, some radio designs did not incorporate the buffer resistor. However, all used the buffer capacitor. Sinc the buffer also acts to reduce sparking at the vibrator contacts, its condition is critical to the reliability of the vibrator. It is a standard rule in the trade that the buffer must always be renewed when the vibrator is renewed. Replace a buffer with another that is as close as possible to the original value. The voltage rating of buffer capacitors will be in the 1200- to 2000-volts dc range.

Fig. 5-12 shows an alternate method used to generate the high-voltage levels demanded by older

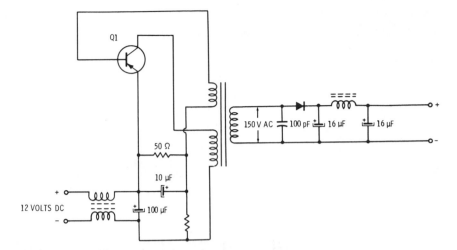

Fig. 5-12. Transistor multivibrator power supply.

tubes. This particular circuit is from the imported (Germany) Blaupunkt Frankfurt model. Basically, this circuit is nothing more than an audio oscillator with a power-transformer primary as its load. Notice the dual primary design of the power transformer. The extra winding is a feedback winding to facilitate oscillation. The high-fre-quency audio oscillations are inductively coupled through the power transformer to the high-voltage secondary and the rectifier circuits. Most frequently, these power supplies use toroid power transformers because of their increased efficiency in this type of service.

Chapter 6

Pushbutton and Manual Tuners

The function of the tuner assembly is to provide a means for the radio user to select the station of his choice with a minimum of effort. In a typical home radio, this function is accomplished by a gang of two or three variable capacitors driven by a dial system. In car radios, however, it is the inductive elements of resonant tank circuits that are varied to select a station.

TUNING SECTION

Fig. 6-1 shows part of a tuning section from an imported car radio. The tuning slugs for each coil are connected to a movable rod called the core bar. The core bar has a threaded hole through which passes a worm gear shaft. The worm gear is driven directly by the manual tuning shaft protruding from the front panel of the radio. The worm gear allows the position of the manual tuning shaft to remain fixed while, at the same time, allowing the core bar to move back and forth. This causes the tuning shaft to indirectly move the tuning cores in and out of their respective coils. For purposes of radio alignment and to insure proper dial-frequency tracking, the precise position of the cores relative to the coils can be varied by turning the small threaded support molded into the ferrite body.

In pushbutton car radios, the core bar is driven even more indirectly. The manual tuning assembly is connected to the treadle bar. The treadle bar is illustrated in Fig. 6-2. The core bar is connected to one of the transverse arms of the treadle by suitable linkage. The treadle rotates about its axis as the manual tuning shaft is turned. This action

pushes the core bar from one position to another, thereby tuning the radio.

Fig. 6-3 shows the gear drive mechanism used to operate the treadle bar. When the clutch is engaged, the clutch facing will press against the clutch disc. Power can then be transferred from the manual tuning shaft to the manual tuning gear. This, in turn, operates the inner shaft, treadle bar, and the tuner core bar. There is frequently a pinion shaft coupling the gear and the manual tuning shaft. In many designs, however, the shaft is all one piece.

Also connected to the outer member of the shaft is a piece called the gating plate. The function of this piece is to move the inner clutch disc far enough to disengage the clutch. This will free the tuner so that a pushbutton assembly can drive the treadle bar. The gating plate is operated by a trip bar that is driven by the individual pushbutton assemblies.

Fig. 6-4 is a photograph of a typical Delco pushbutton tuner mechanism. Although it is a little different from the system just described, the basic functional blocks are the same.

Delco and certain other manufacturers use a clutch system such as that shown in Fig. 6-5. In this system there is no rubber clutch facing. It is essential that the adjustments to the clutch assembly be made properly, or the clutch, and therefore the dial, will slip. There are two machine screws used to make the appropriate adjustments. One of these is accessible to the outer side panel of the radio. The manual tuning gear on the Delco clutch assembly is of the *anti-backlash* type. In this system, two thin regular gears are interfaced. They are held together by a power spring. The spring forces the two halves to attempt to rotate in opposite directions. Should the manual tuning shaft become disengaged, the gear halves will rotate to a

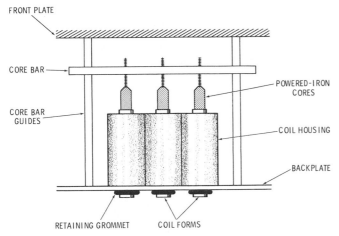

Fig. 6-1. Manual tuning assembly.

rest position. In some models this can occur whenever the front escutcheon is removed from the radio chassis. This situation could arise during many normal service procedures such as changing volume control and so forth. In these cases it will

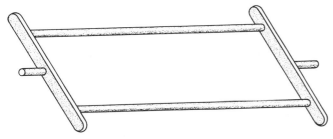

Fig. 6-2. Treadle bar.

be necessary to rerotate the two halves of the antibacklash gear by hand and then re-engage the manual tuning shaft with the gear teeth. The entire assembly must be held in place until the manual tuning shaft can be properly secured.

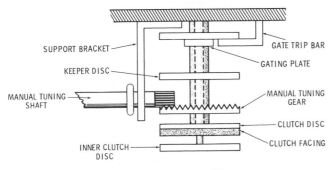

Fig. 6-3. Clutch assembly.

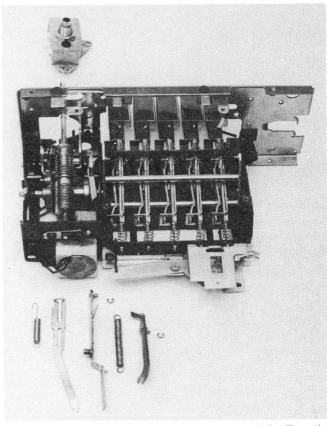

Courtesy Delco Electronics

Fig. 6-4. Delco pushbutton tuner.

DIAL-DRIVE SYSTEM

Fig. 6-6 shows a typical dial-drive system that might be found in a manual tuning radio. This system is not unlike similar dial drives found on many, if not most, home radio receivers. A piece of nylon cord, similar in many respects to fishing line, is run between the manual tuning shaft and three idler wheels. The idlers can actually be either small wheels or solid bearing surfaces. The dial pointer can be secured to the dial cord by glue or pinch tabs. Drive power is supplied by the user when he rotates the manual tuning shaft. To insure proper operation, the cord must be wrapped tightly around the manual tuning shaft for several complete turns. In most systems a small degree of tension is supplied by using a spring to join together the two loose ends of the dial cord. Most radios have a calibration point etched into the dial support plate to tell you where the outer edge of the pointer should be when the tuner is at the low frequency end of its travel.

A more complex dial-drive system used with pushbutton tuners is illustrated in Fig. 6-7. In this

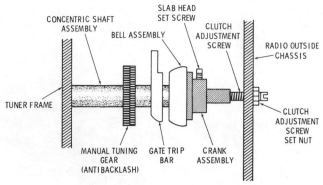

Fig. 6-5. Delco clutch assembly.

arrangement the dial pointer is at the end of a long arm designed so that it can travel the width of the tuner front face. The pointer arm is attached to a movable linkage driven either by the treadle bar or the core bar. In either case, the position of the pointer is controlled by the position of the cores.

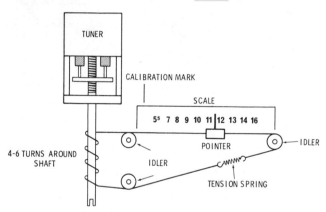

Fig. 6-6. Manual tuner dial drive system.

ADJUSTMENTS

Any technician who is engaged in the repair of car radios will eventually be faced with the necessity of either setting a pushbutton or instructing the customer on how this is done. Except for a few Chrysler products made in the early fifties, all modern car radio pushbuttons are set in the same manner. The station of interest selected by the user is first tuned in manually. It is essential that the station be properly tuned dead center in the middle of the radio passband. The pushbutton that you want to assign to this station is then pulled out (about one-half inch). When the button is pushed all the way back in to the point where you feel it latch, it is programmed. From then on that particular pushbutton should tune the station for which it is set until the user decides that it should be changed.

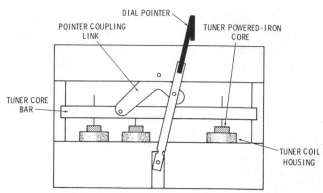

Fig. 6-7. Pushbutton tuner dial-drive system.

In the early Chrysler radios the pushbuttons were connected to the band-switch assembly. There is a screwdriver adjustment immediately beneath a small decorative cap on the front of the button. This adjustment varies the position of the cores in small trimmer coils. This type of pushbutton assembly may reappear in the future if voltage tuning designs become more popular. With a voltage-tuned receiver, the screwdriver adjustment will operate a small potentiometer that changes the level of the dc tuning voltage applied to the variable capacitance diodes. This circuitry already exists in certain home fm stereo hi-fi receivers.

TUNER SERVICING

From time to time it is necessary to service the car radio tuner. Problems occur frequently on pushbutton designs. One recurring complaint is that the manual tuning function does not operate. Normally the problem is an improperly disengaged clutch assembly, caused by a gate bar that is either bent or impeded by dirt. Cleaning or reworking the gate bar should restore normal operation. In older radios the clutch facing, especially the now rarely used cork varieties, may become glazed to a point where no appreciable friction can be developed. In these cases it is necessary to install a new clutch facing—available as part of a kit from most radio-tv parts distributors. In most of these kits, you will find that there is an assortment of sizes and styles costing less than a dollar for a dozen pieces. Another cause of the same symptom is a worn or broken manual tuning shaft. In radios using a pinion made of plastic, this is a common occurrence. In any event, replacement of the defective part is the only proper cure.

Another fairly common symptom is excessive drag or a totally jammed tuner. In these cases, the pushbuttons will be unable to move the dial pointer. It will be necessary to localize the defect before you can determine the cause. To do this, depress one pushbutton about half-way (enough to operate the gate trip bar) and attempt to move the pointer by hand. If it moves freely then you can look to the clutch assembly for the trouble. If the pointer still drags, look at the treadle bar, core bar, or the pointer drive mechanism. There are

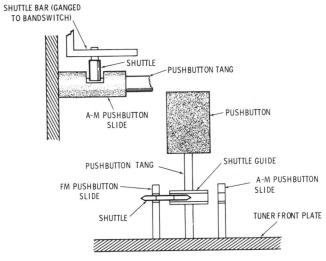

Fig. 6-8. Bendix 10-slide tuner.

two main causes of drag and jams in the tuner assembly. The first is dirt and corrosion under the various moving surfaces. Another is misadjustment of either the clutch assembly or the treadle-bar side bearing. In the latter instance you may find a small set screw on the side frame plate of the tuner. At the inside end of the screw, there will

be either a tip or ball bearing to ride against the treadle bar bearing. If the pressure of this screw against the treadle bar is excessive, overall drag will increase to a point where the pushbuttons are either difficult or impossible to operate.

Major defects in tuners must sometimes be corrected by replacing the entire assembly. This can be quite expensive—make sure the radio is worth it before proceeding. You may experience difficulty in obtaining the correct tuner from the manufacturer's parts department. Often car radios are found bearing the same make and model designations yet may contain completely different tuner assemblies. There are several basic tuners available. Most will be marked either *TRW* or *GIC*. Be sure to include these tuner frame markings on the parts order. Some manufacturers have been getting around this problem by sending the entire front escutcheon. Replacement is then easier, since you change the entire front casting.

A new style tuner that has appeared only during the past few years is the *10-slide* design used on am/fm radios by Bendix and Delco. Most pushbutton tuners have only five or six buttons (and slides). These must be split up between the two bands. The 10-slide tuner makes use of all five buttons on both bands by utilizing a split-slide design. Small selectors on each pushbutton assembly determine which slide is in use at any particular time. These selectors are transferred from one gang of slides to the other by a shuttle bar that that is ganged to the am/fm bandswitch mechanical linkage (Fig. 6-8).

Chapter 7

Signal-Seeking Tuners

Modern communication congestion has made the signal-seeking tuner a popular option on car radios. Delco introduced the signal seeker under the trade name *Wonder Bar* in the early fifties. A recent-model Delco *Wonder Bar* radio is shown in Fig. 7-1. Although the Delco design has changed somewhat over the years, the mechanical portion is essentially the same as it was almost two decades ago. Most of the mechanical changes have represented sophistication, improvement, and a trend toward compactness rather than radical departures from the basic concept. The design has proved so durable that both Bendix and Becker *AutoRadio* (German) have used signal seekers with similar designs in some of their radios. Another design uses a dc motor to drive the tuner mechanism. This design, however, has faded from the scene. The few radios using the motor-driven type of seeker are being produced in Japan.

The basic job of the signal-seeking tuner is to drive the radio dial and Permeability Tuning Mechanism (PTM) from one end of the band to the other, while allowing it to stop on any station which has a signal strength above a certain preset threshold level. A properly working signal seeker will stop on the exact center of a station so that the operator will not have to manually tune the set for best reception.

TRAVELING RACK

Fig. 7-2 shows two illustrations of a partially disassembled Delco *Wonder Bar* mechanism from a recent-model am/fm radio. The actual PTM portion of the tuner is similar to the regular pushbutton tuner discussed in a previous chapter. The added features that make this a signal seeker are the spring-powered traveling rack and additional worm gear. When the seek cycle is initiated, the clutch assembly disengages so that the treadle bar (7-2B) is free to move. The front worm gear on the traveling rack assembly is engaged to the anti-backlash gear mounted to the clutch. This allows the rack to rotate the treadle bar and thereby advance the core bar from the low end of the band toward the high end. The power spring supplies the energy needed to drag the traveling rack from the rear end of its support rod to the front end.

GOVERNOR

If allowed to move freely, the rack would travel too fast to be of any use. It would cover the distance between the two ends of the dial in less than a second. Even the best stopping circuit could not react that fast. Besides that, there has to be some practical way to halt the rack or the whole purpose of a signal seeker is thwarted. To accomplish both speed regulation and stopping functions, Delco has designed a gear-train governor, as shown in Fig. 7-3 (housing removed). The largest diameter gear in the train is engaged to the rack via the drive spline. This gear is also coupled to the paddle wheel via the second gear. Concentric to the paddle wheel shaft is a centrifugal drag mechanism. This drag device has a pair of wings that expand from their rest position as the rotational speed increases. This increases the drag (against the inside of its metal housing) and slows down the speed of the entire chain of gears. If the speed of the rack causes the gear train to speed up, the drag will increase to a point that will counteract the rack so

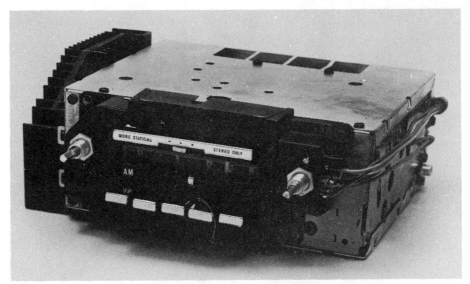

Fig. 7-1. Recent-model Delco *Wonder Bar* radio.

Courtesy Delco Electronics

that the whole mechanism slows down. If, on the other hand, the speed of the mechanism slows down a bit, the drag reduces enough to compensate. The action of the governor causes the speed of the rack to remain within relatively narrow limits predetermined by the design of the gear train. The speed regulation function of the governor is only effective when the rack is traveling in the forward direction. In the reverse direction, drag is at a minimum so that the signal seeker can be recocked easily.

The stop function is provided by the paddle wheel inside the governor housing. A hole is drilled through the body of the gear train so that access can be gained to the paddle wheel. As seen in the insert of Fig. 7-4, the armature of a sensitive relay (K1) is fitted with a tang. This tang fits into the hole to engage the paddle wheel. When the relay is in a de-energized position, the tang is engaged with the paddle wheel in such a way that the whole mechanism is stopped. At the start of the seek cycle, the relay becomes energized. The tang pulls out of the governor, and the power spring moves the rack forward. The relay will de-energize and stop the mechanism when the trigger circuit encounters a strong signal.

RECOCK SOLENOID

When the signal seeker reaches the high-frequency end of the dial, both the spring and the PTM must be recocked. To accomplish this function there is a solenoid and plunger that pull the rack, power spring, and PTM to the low-frequency end (low end) position. A sliding plate

ganged to the treadle bar is used to activate the switch that supplies power to the solenoid. This plate is also returned to the low-end position by the action of the solenoid plunger. When it reaches the low end position, the sliding plate turns off the solenoid power. This solenoid draws 16 amperes during the recock cycle. This heavy load necessitates using a high-quality power supply for bench servicing. Use of a lower-quality supply may cause the solenoid to jam during recock. Should the jam occur before the power switch is turned off, the solenoid will burn up due to the heavy current.

TRIGGER SECTION

Before proceeding to our discussion of the trigger section let's review the mechanical sequence of events. The relay is energized by the operator initiating the seek cycle. This frees the governor, so that the power spring can propel the traveling rack forward. Constant speed is maintained by the drag of the governor assembly. The rack moves the treadle bar, thereby tuning the radio. When a station is encountered, the trigger circuit de-energizes the relay. The relay tang falls back into its place in the control hole of the governor and stops the movement of the rack.

Fig. 7-5 shows the trigger section from a typical Delco (nonstereo) signal seeker. Relay K1 controls the paddle wheel in the governor and serves to activate both the trigger and sensitivity determining circuits. To initiate the seek cycle, the user depresses the *Wonder Bar* on the front of the radio, which closes switch S1. With S1 closed, current can flow through the windings of the control relay

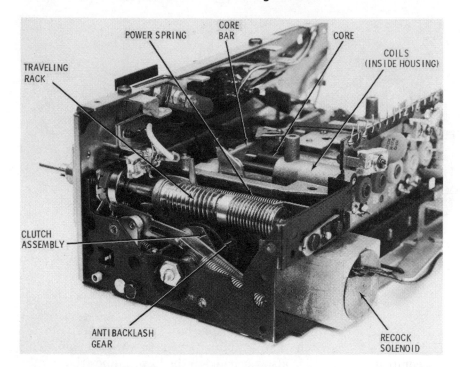

(A) *Side view.*

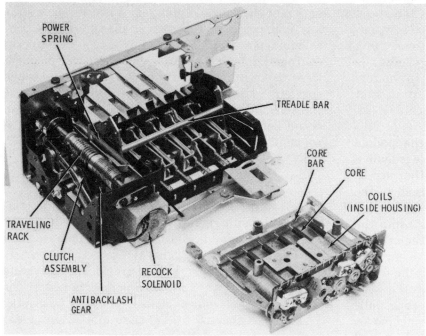

(B) *View exposing the treadle bar.*

Courtesy Delco Electronics

Fig. 7-2. Partially disassembled Delco *Wonder Bar* radio.

(K1). This current causes K1 to pull in and activate Q2 and Q3. Also, the tang pulls out of the governor when K1 is energized, and the traveling rack begins moving. The radio is in search of a station.

In order to prevent power-supply voltage variation that could cause the signal seeker to de-energize, there is a zener diode (CR1) shunting the power line leading to the trigger section. This power line is used to furnish both collector voltage and forward-bias to Q2, the relay amplifier transistor. The collector-emitter current resulting from the forward-bias applied to Q2 causes a voltage drop to appear across its 2200-ohm emitter resistor. Since the emitter of Q2 is directly coupled to the base of Q3, the emitter-resistor voltage drop acts to forward bias Q3. When forward-biased, Q3 will begin to conduct current. Relay K1 requires a somewhat larger current to pull in than it needs to

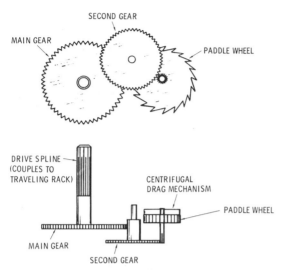

Fig. 7-3. Gear-train governor (housing removed).

stay in the energized position. Because of this, the smaller current flowing through the 1500-ohm collector load resistor and the collector of Q3 is sufficient to keep the relay energized until the trigger amplifier tells it to drop out.

A-M STOP FUNCTION

The Delco design uses two signal samples (Fig. 7-6) to insure the accuracy of the stop function on a-m. One signal is taken from the collector circuit of the a-m i-f amplifier transistor and flows down through R1 and R2 to B+. The second signal (the larger of the two) flows through R1 also. It is the interaction of these two signals that insures accuracy. The waveshape of these two signals, as well as the resultant, is shown graphically in Fig. 7-7. The T2 primary signal is shown as curve B and the T2 secondary signal is shown at curve A. The resultant signal, shown at C, is impressed on the base of the trigger amplifier transistor. This transistor is operated immediately below its cutoff point. The resultant added to the fixed bias, is sufficient to cause the trigger amplifier transistor to conduct heavily, placing the collector of Q1 at approximately ground potential. When the seek function was first started, capacitor C1 (Fig. 7-5) had charged up to a high potential (positive on the collector of Q1 and negative on the base of Q2). This voltage did not affect Q2 since Q1 was essentially an open circuit at that time. However, when a signal is received that causes Q1 to conduct heavily, the positive side of C1 becomes grounded (through

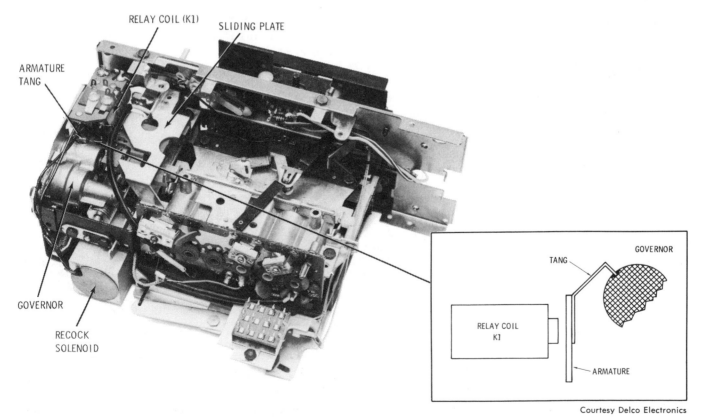

Courtesy Delco Electronics

Fig. 7-4. The armature tang of the tuner operating relay fits into the governor.

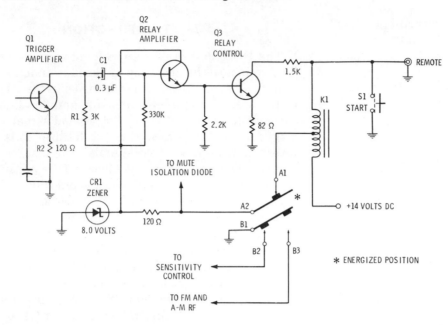

Fig. 7-5. Trigger section of a typical Delco signal seeker (nonstereo circuitry).

Q1 and R2). The base of the relay amplifier will become very negative with respect to ground, and thus highly negative with respect to the emitter.

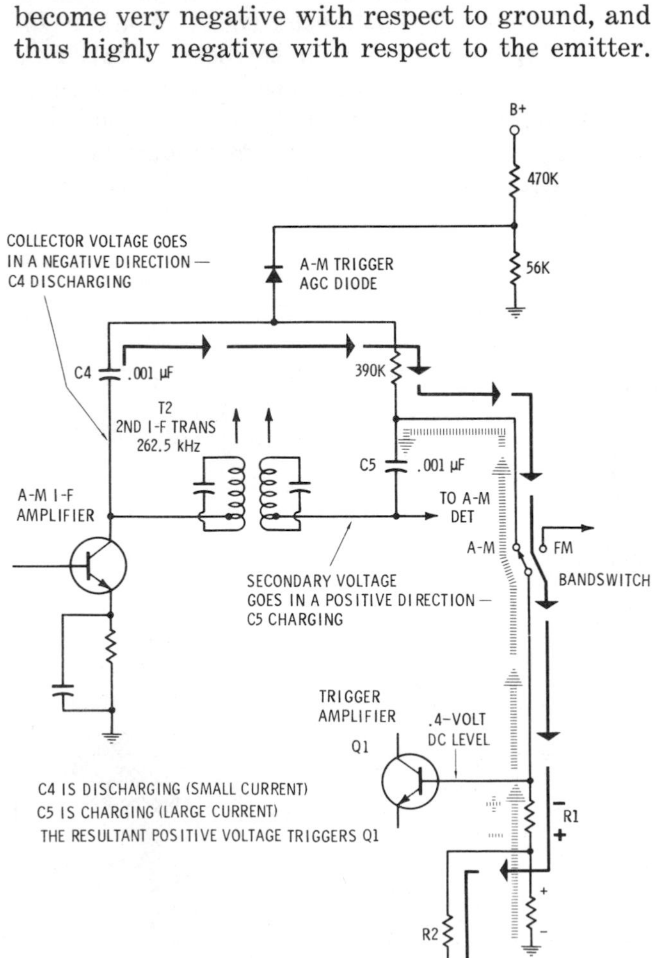

The preceding action cuts Q2 off very fast. With Q2 in a cutoff state, there will be no conduction current to cause a voltage drop across the 2200-ohm emitter resistor. The loss of this voltage causes the relay control transistor to cease conducting. With its ground path open, K1 becomes de-energized. This causes the armature tang to fall back into place, where it stops the action of the governor. The relay de-energizes at point 1, and the tang finally stops at point 2—hopefully dead-on center station.

FM STOP FUNCTION

Fig. 7-8 is a schematic of an fm stopping circuit. A 10.7-MHz square wave is passed from the

COLLECTOR VOLTAGE GOES
IN A NEGATIVE DIRECTION —
C4 DISCHARGING

SECONDARY VOLTAGE
GOES IN A POSITIVE DIRECTION —
C5 CHARGING

C4 IS DISCHARGING (SMALL CURRENT)
C5 IS CHARGING (LARGE CURRENT)
THE RESULTANT POSITIVE VOLTAGE TRIGGERS Q1

Fig. 7-6. Obtaining the trigger voltage for Q1.

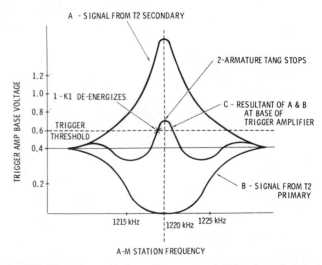

Fig. 7-7. Waveshape of the collector signal (T2 primary) versus the T2 secondary signal, and the resulting trigger signal.

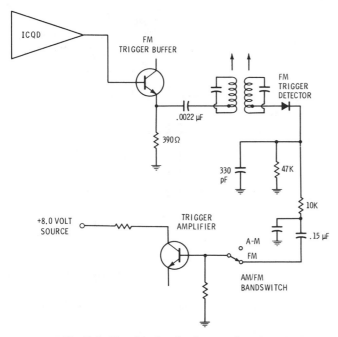

Fig. 7-8. Circuitry for the fm stop function.

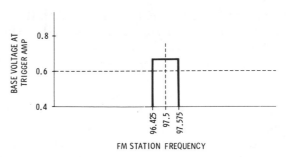

Fig. 7-9. The output of the ICQD.

integrated-circuit quadrature detector (ICQD) through a various circuitry to a trigger detector diode. The signal from the diode charges the .15-μF capacitor rapidly. This potential pushes the trigger amplifier transistor over the threshold and into a conducting state. From then on, the action is the same as for the a-m stop cycle. The .3-μF capacitor discharges, throwing a negative-going pulse to the base of the relay amplifier. The extreme sharpness of the square-wave output from the ICQD (Fig. 7-9) eliminates the

need for the fancy stopping accuracy measures taken on a-m. In early fm signal seekers which used either discriminators or ratio detectors, such measures were used. The newer ICQD, however, eliminates the necessity of such circuitry.

STEREO SIGNAL SEEKERS

Newer fm signal seekers are designed to receive and decode stereo programs. Unfortunately, not all fm stations transmit stereo. For those who wish the signal seeker to stop only on stereo stations, there is a special position of the sensitivity switch. The trigger amplifier in these sets operates exactly as in nonstereo am/fm signal seekers. There is, however, one added transistor that causes the circuit to function as an AND gate. An AND gate is a circuit that gives an output only when all inputs (in this case two) are present. In Fig. 7-10, we see a trigger amplifier and trigger control transistor. Transistor Q2 is connected in series between the emitter of Q1 and ground—Q2 must be for-

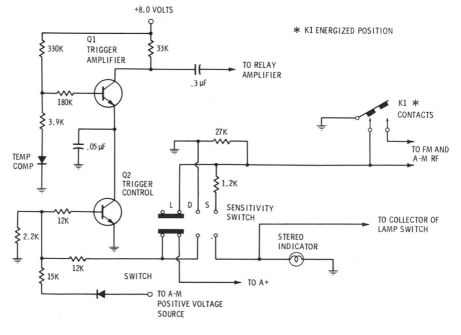

Fig. 7-10. Trigger amplifier and control for a stereo signal seeker.

59

ward-biased before Q1 can operate. With the trigger control transistor forward-biased, the trigger amplifier sees almost the same situation as it did when there was a 120-ohm emitter resistor in the circuit (nonstereo radios).

In either a-m or regular fm modes, the trigger control transistor will be forward-biased as long as the sensitivity switch is in any position other than "stereo only." Should the sensitivity switch be in the "stereo only" position (position S) while the radio bandswitch is set to the "a-m" position, the trigger control transistor is still forward-biased because its base network is connected to the a-m positive voltage source. Under these conditions, the trigger amplifier will operate normally. When the bandswitch is set to the "fm" position and the sensitivity switch is set to the "stereo only" position, the trigger amplifier can only respond to fm stereo signals. The trigger amplifier will continue to receive signals from the fm trigger detector, but they will be unable to pass unless Q2 is forward-biased. The necessary forward bias is obtained from the stereo indicator lamp. This lamp turns on to let the operator know when he is tuned to a stereo station. The voltage applied to the lamp is also applied, through the sensitivity switch, to the base of Q2. This voltage saturates Q2, making it little more than a low-value resistor, in relation to the emitter circuit of Q1.

Signal-seeking circuits may not respond to low-level signals. The audio amplifiers, however, will respond to these signals. The result is that the listener will hear these weak signals as the tuner sweeps past them. To eliminate this annoying effect most signal seekers incorporate a mute or squelch circuit to silence the audio amplifiers during the seek cycle. Fig. 7-11 shows a typical mute circuit from a Delco *Wonder Bar* radio. When the control relay is energized, a positive voltage is applied to the anode of the mute isolation diode. This voltage has two functions: it reverse-biases the a-m detector diode so that no signal will pass, and it clamps the audio preamplifier transistor in a saturated mode. This keeps any incoming audio signal from entering the audio preamplifier. When the seeker finds a station, relay K1 de-energizes. This removes the muting voltage so that both the detector and audio amplifier can once again function in a normal manner.

Recent Delco radios using ceramic module (DM-8 or DM-28) audio stages have a similar system to provide muting. Fig. 7-12 shows the muting circuit for one of these sets. A positive voltage applied to pin 4 of the DM-8 module causes

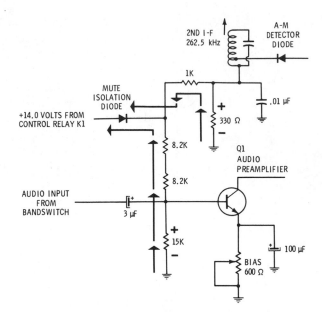

Fig. 7-11. Typical Delco mute circuit from a *Wonder Bar* radio.

the same action as in the regular audio circuit. The ceramic modules are isolated from the power supply by the same sort of diode used in the conventional circuit. A pair of resistors supplies the squelch voltage to the appropriate terminal of the module. When the relay de-energizes, the squelch voltage disappears, and operation returns to normal.

Sometimes signal seekers tend to find too many stations. They may, for example, stop immediately when the *Wonder Bar* is released because of either too many stations or too much noise. In some sea-coast areas, the signal seeker may appear unable to restart on a-m after the solenoid has recocked the power spring and returned the tuner to the low

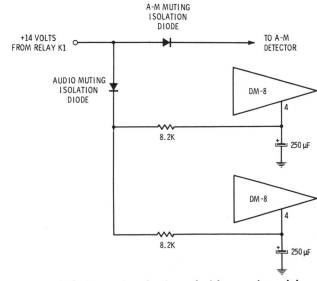

Fig. 7-12. Delco muting circuit used with ceramic modules.

end of the dial. This may be due to the trigger circuit responding to very weak marine continuous-wave (cw) signals. These signals are generated for maritime communications with shore stations. There is no modulation present, so they will appear on an a-m car radio as an intermittent but rhythmic hissing sound. Since car radio tweet filters attenuate much of the high-frequency component of this hiss, it becomes only barely audible in the output. The trigger circuit, however, responds to the i-f signal rather than the audio signal. The cw is strong enough in that section of the radio to fire the trigger yet remain almost inaudible to the listener. To test for this type of defect, try injecting a weak, unmodulated signal into the i-f amplifier. Use a frequency close to 262.5 kHz. A 263-kHz signal, for example, will beat with the unknown to produce a 500-Hz heterodyne output. If the seeker stops at the low end of the a-m band and this test indicates the presence of a signal that sounds something like "beep bip beep beep beep beep bip beep," you have found the defect. In these cases, a minor realignment is indicated. The response is caused by misalignment of the local oscillator frequency. The marine cw calling and emergency channel is at 500 kHz. The radio should only tune down as far as 540 kHz. If the radio is responding to these signals, then the local oscillator must be shifted higher in frequency by at least 40 kHz. This problem can, by the way, be rather difficult to those who are not used to troubleshooting signal seekers in areas where marine signals are relatively strong.

Another quick test to reveal the existence of a barely audible signal on the low end of the band is to set the sensitivity switch to the local position. This reduces the sensitivity of the radio by altering the bias conditions in the rf amplifiers (Fig. 7-13). When relay contacts B1, B2, and B3 are shorted together (relay K1 de-energized), the emitter resistors of the a-m and fm rf amplifiers return to ground as usual. During the seek cycle, however, these contacts open, requiring their respective emitter currents to flow through the sensitivity switch. This switch will either return the emitters directly to ground or will route their currents through one or two series resistors. The sensitivity switch is especially useful in large metropolitan areas where there are a large number of stations and at night when skip signals seem to multiply the number of available stations. These skip signals arrive from distant cities and from foreign countries. (Many Spanish-speaking stations may be heard on the a-m broadcast band.)

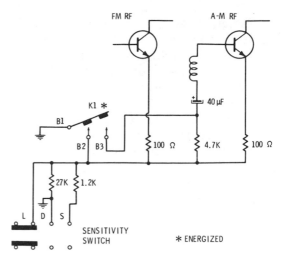

Fig. 7-13. Sensitivity switch alters bias on rf amplifiers.

TYPICAL SERVICE PROBLEMS

It is important for a technician to have knowledge of the previous failures of a unit before he attempts to service that unit. Both time and money can be saved if the technician has this knowledge. A few typical problems with signal seekers are listed below for your benefit.

Failure to Recock

When the traveling rack comes to the front end of its run, a small leaf switch is tripped to fire the recock solenoid. Any defect that causes a failure in the solenoid circuit or its mechanical linkage will result in a failure to recock. One very common class of defects involves the recock switch. If this switch is open (Fig. 7-14), no current can flow through the solenoid magnet windings. The test for this is to energize the seeker, and then momentarily ground the solenoid wire where it enters the switch. If the switch is defective then the solenoid will fire correctly. Another common defect involv-

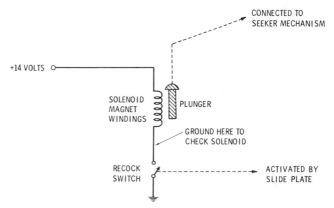

Fig. 7-14. The recock switch is in series with the solenoid windings.

ing the switch is failure to toggle. The toggle arm of the switch is activated by a sliding plate ganged to the treadle bar. If the sliding plate is binding due to dirt or warpage, or if it is misadjusted, it will not be able to operate the recock switch.

Mechanical jams in the linkage attached to the solenoid plunger can also cause a failure to recock. In these instances, the solenoid will fire but the dial and tuner will jam half-way through the recock cycle. Although such jams could be any place in the linkage, one good place to start is the clutch gate. The clutch must be free during recocking. A gate bar used to separate the clutch sections is operated by the solenoid plunger. Also, check to be sure that the treadle bar is free to move. Slightly depress one of the manual pushbuttons and try moving the treadle bar by hand. It should offer only a small amount of drag.

Many of the battery-eliminator power supplies advertised for car radio use have neither the regulation nor the current capacity for signal-seeker service. The recock solenoid requires 16 amperes during the recock. If the output voltage of the power supply drops appreciably during the cycle, then the solenoid will hang up half-way through its travel. The switch used to turn the solenoid on and off is turned off at the end of the recock cycle. When the solenoid hangs up due to underpower, the turn-off will not operate and the solenoid will burn. This solenoid can carry the 16-ampere load only for a short period. Longer periods exceed the duty factor. If your power supply causes this type of problem you may alleviate the situation by running the voltage up to well over 16 volts. This can only be done, however, for extremely short periods of time because the power-supply filters and all of the other electrical components are designed for operation at a voltage less than 16 volts. An alternative is to connect the battery eliminator (charger-style) in parallel with an automobile storage battery.

Machine Gunning

As mentioned earlier in this chapter, the only thing that keeps the traveling rack from traveling at a high rate of speed is the retarding effect of the governor gear train. Should the governor become inoperative through misadjustment, a stripped gear, or other defect, the rack will slam forward and strike the front stop. This triggers the recock solenoid. The solenoid whips the rack back to the low end of the dial rapidly. Since the governor is defective, the rack will once again slam forward at a high rate of speed. This action will go on as long

as power is applied to the seeker circuits. The outward symptoms are a *machine gun* sound and a rapid movement of the dial back and forth across the band. Readjustment of the governor, or installing a new governor if the old is defective, is the cure. Do not take too long a look at these symptoms, as machine gunning can cause damage to other parts of the seeker mechanism. Most frequently, the dial pointer will break off if the machine gunning continues too long.

Failure to Seek

Another type of defect frequently seen on signal seekers is a failure to seek. In most cases the relay will energize but the mechanism remains stationary. The cause is usually a jam somewhere in the mechanism. One possible jam point is the clutch gate bar; another is the bearings supporting the treadle bar. A third, but by no means the last, is either a frozen or misadjusted governor. In older radios, it may be necessary to clean and lubricate the seeker mechanism. The support rod for the traveling rack often has a felt *oil reservoir* washer fixed at one end. Make sure that this washer is slightly dampened with a good grade of light sewing machine oil. Do not excessively distribute the oil, or it will wind up covering everything in the radio.

In cases where the signal seeker simply will not start, look for either a defective *Wonder Bar* switch or an open control relay. If the radio mutes properly, then these parts will most likely be in good shape. If it fails to mute and refuses to run, then the switch and relay are the suspect. This relay can operate normally yet still fail to mute the receiver output. In these cases the probable difficulty is an open muting diode.

Failure to Stop

This is probably the most common defect. The relay energizes, the seeker mechanism runs at the proper speed, and the radio mutes. But the seeker will not stop on any station. An obvious fault might be a shorted *Wonder Bar* switch. This is especially likely if the radio is equipped with a remote switch. These switches are located on the floor boards adjacent to the headlight dimmer switch. In some models, especially the limousines, there is a remote switch for the use of rear seat passengers. In cars using one of the remote seeker switches, the short can be in the jack at the radio, the connecting cable, or the switches. A short in any of the start switches will cause the radio to stay in the seek mode.

When the radio operates normally until the seeker switch is depressed, yet will fail to stop on any station, it is unlikely that the switch is at fault. There are several possible problem areas that could cause this symptom. One is radio sensitivity. Check the sensitivity either by measurement or by an *air* check. It is a good idea to find a semilocal station to use for this purpose. Find a station that becomes audible only when the antenna trimmer on the radio is properly peaked. This station will be inaudible if there is a defect in the radio. Although somewhat idealized and rather subjective, this method does offer a quick check on radio sensitivity—at least for service applications.

Electrical defects in the trigger amplifier or the directly coupled relay transistors can also cause a seeker to keep running. An open transistor, for example, is one such defect. If any of the coupling capacitors are open, you can also expect these symptoms.

If a seeker fails to stop on center station, a customer will come looking for service. On a-m, the probable cause is loss of one of the two trigger signals. An open coupling capacitor or trigger agc diode will cause this effect. On fm, it will probably be a trigger transformer that is either defective or misadjusted. Misaligned trigger transformers are especially likely in older designs. It can, however, also occur in the newer ICQD sets.

Besides the adjustments for stopping accuracy, there is little that the service technician need bother about in the electrical portion of the signal-seeker radio. The mechanical portion does, however, require occasional adjustment. The tension of the treadle bar and the clutch assembly may be adjusted the same as on a regular pushbutton tuner. The governor is adjusted so that the mechanism runs smoothly. Another adjustment requiring attention is the solenoid switch. This switch is turned on and off by the sliding plate at the high end of the band. Frequently, it is necessary to bend the tabs that operate this switch so solenoid turn-on and turn-off occur at the proper times. When operating properly, the seeker will run smoothly. Even minor defects can appear as relatively radical symptoms. It is then that the car radio repairman may show his talents.

Chapter 8

Tape-Player Motor Circuits

Speed regulation is the key to success in tape-drive systems. The reduction of frequency modulation (wow and flutter) and overall quality of audio reproduction are directly related to the degree of speed regulation designed into any particular machine. It is speed regulation, and how well it is handled, that can make or break a tape-player design.

SPEED REGULATION

The simplest motor used in the lower-priced eight-track and cassette machines employs an internal governor switch to directly control speed. This type of motor is generally referred to as *two-wire*. Such a motor is illustrated in Fig. 8-1. The switch is a centrifugal type mounted to the rotor of the motor. The contacts on this switch open when the rotational speed of the motor reaches a certain preset threshold level. An example of a centrifugal switch is shown on top of an armature in Fig. 8-2. Often, there is a means of adjusting the throw-out point of the switch. This adjustment is a small counterweight screw attached to the switch mount. On motors where an adjustment is permitted, there will be a small access hole drilled into the motor casing. In most cases, this hole will be covered either by a piece of tape or by a section of adhesive-backed label paper. Any speed variations outside the limits of the counterweight screw must be corrected by replacement of the entire motor. Occasional defects such as contact pitting occur and cause the motor to run wildly at a high rate of speed. This is due to the centrifugal switch contacts sticking together. The most obvious, but not always the most successful cure is to burnish the switch contact facings. Use either a burnishing tool or matchbook cover.

The three-wire motor circuit offers somewhat improved control over speed variations. In the simplest circuits utilizing the three-wire motor, a time constant determined by an RC network is used to regulate the motor. Such a circuit, typical of many Japanese imports, is shown in Fig. 8-3. The values of the resistor and capacitor are semicritical. If any parts are replaced, it is necessary to use a value as close to the original as possible. Should a parts availability problem require the substitution of a near value, it may be necessary to vary the value of another component to compensate for the change in the RC time constant.

A related version of this type of regulator circuit is shown in Fig. 8-4. This four-wire motor circuit was used in the Delco T-200 series tape players. Notice that this circuit uses a suppression diode to reduce the inductive kick caused by the motor winding when the centrifugal switch opens. This diode can be incorporated into some nonDelco designs of similar nature to prolong the life of newly burnished switch contacts. Both the diode and the iron-core choke reduce the intensity of the hash generated by the motor circuit.

There are several problems common to most RC regulated or simple two-wire switch controlled tape-drive systems. One of these is extremely fast running. The main cause of this symptom is pitted switch contacts. An open RC network capacitor can also cause dramatic changes of speed. A slow-running motor can sometimes be traced to either a defective RC network component or to a binding drive system. Before replacing any drive-system part, be sure to clean the capstan, its housing, and

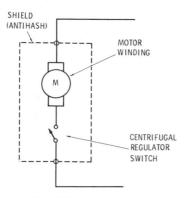

Fig. 8-1. Two-wire motor.

any bearing surfaces being used. It is also considered a good idea to replace the drive belts. Rubber and plastic belts age rapidly and will probably be out of tolerance by the time the player needs other service work performed. Most professional tape player technicians make it a habit to replace the drive belts as a standard operating procedure.

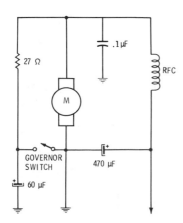

Fig. 8-2. Centrifugal switch on top of motor armature.

The more expensive tape players use a transistor circuit to control motor speed variations. These players usually have a tighter degree of regulation than do less costly two-wire and RC regulated ma-

Fig. 8-3. Simple RC network speed regulator.

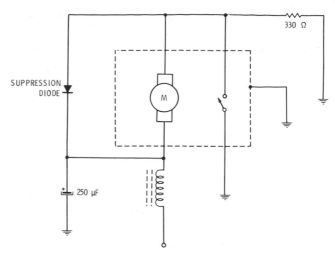

Fig. 8-4. Delco T-200 motor circuit.

chines. Motorola was one of the earliest manufacturers to come out with a transistor regulator circuit. Such an early Motorola circuit is shown in Fig. 8-5. The regulator contacts inside the motor housing are used to either forward bias or remove bias from the transistor circuit as commanded by the centrifugal governor switch. When the contacts are closed, Q1 (Fig. 8-5) is cut off. The switch shorts together the base and emitter terminals of Q1. This causes conduction current to drop

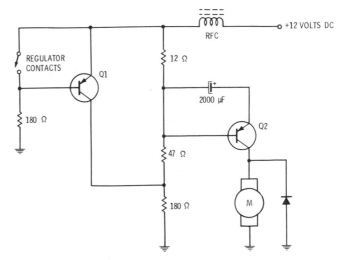

Fig. 8-5. Early-model Motorola transistor regulator circuit.

to zero. The main regulator transistor (Q2) is forward-biased. This causes Q2 to develop a greater collector to ground voltage across the winding of the motor. The motor speeds up to a point where the regulator switch reopens. With the switch open, Q1 is forward-biased. As Q1 conducts, the biasing current to Q2 is lowered. Since Q2 conducts less, the voltage developed across the motor winding is less. With the lower voltage, the motor is forced to slow down. In actuality, the motor is oscillating back and forth across the correct speed.

Tape-player transistor regulators underwent a change from the early Motorola and Lear-Jet multiple transistor designs to simpler, yet equally effective, single transistor designs. All the more recent circuits (until the Delco tachometer design came into being) use only one control transistor. An example of one of the transitional circuits is shown in Fig. 8-6. In this circuit, Motorola has used a 2N176 power transistor as the active control element in the motor speed regulator circuit. The switch in the motor acts to either forward bias or cut off the transistor base-emitter junction. This circuit has been one of the most reliable.

Now, Motorola tape players, especially some of those made for the Ford Motor Company, use the regulator circuit of Fig. 8-7. Although the configuration is somewhat different from that of Fig. 8-6, it is essentially a similar design. The chief difference from the servicer's point of view is that the transistor is being used as the regulator. Almost the entire regulator circuit will be found mounted on a small printed-circuit board close to the rear chassis panel in most of the radio/tape combination units. The most common defect in these circuits is an open regulator transistor. The player will either remain inert when an eight-track cartridge is inserted, or it will start only for a very brief instant. Care must be exercised when handling this or any other plastic power transistor.

Fig. 8-8 shows a related circuit used by Philips, Ltd. of Canada in the radio/tape-player combination units offered by Chrysler in 1969–71. The SJE276 regulator transistor is physically identical to the Motorola transistor of Fig. 8-7. Electrical similarity is so close that most shops use the two types interchangeably. One difference worthy of

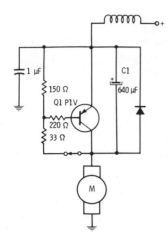

Fig. 8-7. Motorola regulator circuit.

note is the relative location of the motor windings in the two circuits. The Philips design grounds the collector of the regulator transistor, while the Motorola version does not. In the Philips design the motor winding is connected between the power supply and the emitter of the transistor. Motorola, on the other hand, connects the winding between the collector and ground.

Delco tape players in the T-400 series of models are found in a number of General Motors automobiles dating from the late sixties. These players use an npn type DS-509 silicon transistor (Fig. 8-9) in the motor regulator circuit. The regulator switch contacts are used to apply bias (a positive voltage) to the base of the DS-509. This will, of course, forward-bias the transistor and cause it to conduct. With the DS-509 conducting more heavily, the

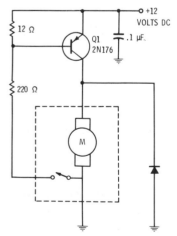

Fig. 8-6. Transitional regulator circuit.

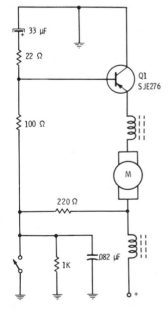

Fig. 8-8. A Philips, Ltd. regulator circuit.

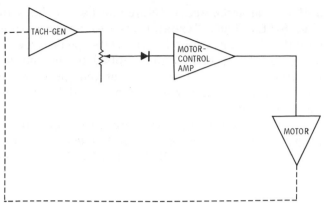

Fig. 8-11. Delco T-400 (block diagram) tachometer-design speed regulator.

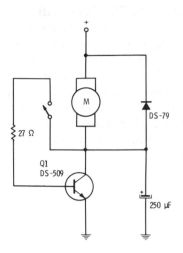

Fig. 8-9. Delco T-400 regulator circuit.

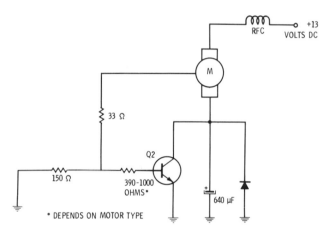

Fig. 8-10. Motorola regulator circuit using an npn transistor.

motor speed will increase. When the switch contacts reopen at a predetermined speed, the transistor will cut off to allow the motor to slow down.

Motorola has switched to an npn transistor in its motor regulator circuit. This newer design is shown in Fig. 8-10. This particular transistor is one of the tab-mounted plastic epoxy types, which is a departure from the earlier plastic style.

One of the most advanced tape-player motor circuits is the tachometer design used by Delco in the later T-400 series tape player and radio/tape player combination units. A block diagram of this arrangement is shown in Fig. 8-11. The motor is a little unusual compared to the simpler motors used in other brands. This motor has both a motor and an ac alternator mounted inside a common case

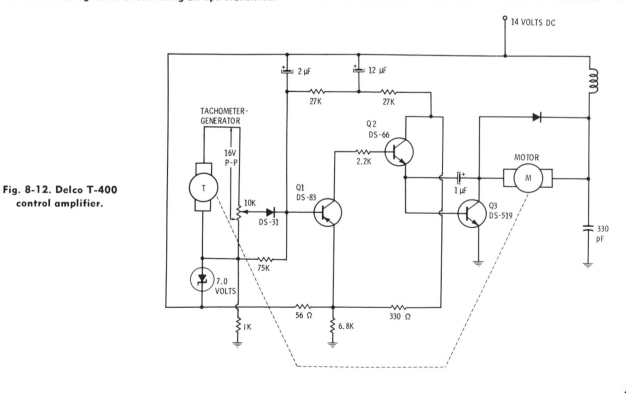

Fig. 8-12. Delco T-400 control amplifier.

and on the same shaft (Note the dashed lines in Fig. 8-11.) The alternator creates an ac output signal of approximately 16 volts peak-to-peak. This signal is rectified and applied to the control amplifier. The amplifier regulates the speed of the motor in accordance with the signal delivered by the alternator.

Fig. 8-12 shows the actual circuit of the control amplifier used in the later T-400 Delco tape players. The motor is controlled by the DS-519 transis-tor designated Q3. This is not unlike the configuration used by many other types of tape players, including earlier T-400 models. The base-emitter circuit of DS-519 is used as the emitter-to-ground load for Q2. Transistor Q1 is used to control Q2. The base circuit of Q2 is the collector load of Q1. Transistor Q1 is controlled directly by the output of the rectified alternator. Since Q1 is a pnp transistor, as the alternator output increases, Q1 will conduct less.

Chapter 9

Eight-Track and Cassette Mechanisms

Since its introduction in the mid-sixties, the eight-track tape cartridge has remained a popular accessory to an automotive electronic entertainment system. In recent years, however, the eight-track system has seen increased competition from cassette systems. In this chapter we will examine the mechanisms and unique circuitry for both systems.

EIGHT-TRACK SYSTEM

Fig. 9-1 shows the active elements of the eight-tape cartridge. It is of the endless loop design. This feature is convenient for automotive use because a great deal of programing can be played with little attention from the driver. The tape in an eight-track cartridge is of the standard quarter-inch size. It has, by virtue of the head design, eight parallel tracks recorded in the same direction. As the cartridge sits horizontally, the tracks are numbered one through eight from the top down. Since stereo requires two tracks simultaneously, program number one will use tracks one and five, program two uses tracks two and six, program three tracks three and seven, and program four uses tracks four and eight. The frequency response of the eight-track system is limited to some degree by the narrowness of the individual tracks. Crosstalk between programs can be a problem because there is only .025 inch of guard space between tracks.

Motor Drive Systems

Fig. 9-2 shows the active elements of the eight-track player as viewed through the cartridge loading slot. The object on the far left is the automatic

program changing switch. This switch consists of a pair of parallel metal plates that run in direct contact with the tape surface. Eight-track cartridges use a strip of adhesive-backed metal foil to splice together the ends of the continuous loop. This foil is used to short together the metal plates of the automatic program switch at the end of each program. This actuates the track-changing mechanism that selects the next program in line.

Next to the automatic program switch is the playback head. This head is a specially designed type made for eight-track service. It is fortunate that around eighty percent of all eight-track players use approximately the same size playback head. This greatly simplifies the parts stock needed. One common size, available from an almost endless variety of sources, will substitute for the original head in the vast majority of machines. The power switch shown in the illustration is resting right next to the head. This is one part of the system that may be found almost anyplace in the machine. The only real requirement is that it be operated when a cartridge is inserted into the loading slot. The last object in the diagram is the tape-drive capstan and its associated bearing housing. The capstan provides the mechanical drive for the tape. It rides in direct contact with the pinch roller inside the cartridge. The principal difference between the eight-track cartridge and the now obsolete four-track cartridge is the capstan pinch-roller arrangement. In the eight-track system, each cartridge has its own self-contained pinch roller. The four-track cartridge, on the other hand, used an external pinch roller mounted to the player. When a four-track cartridge was inserted into the loading slot, the pinch roller was forced

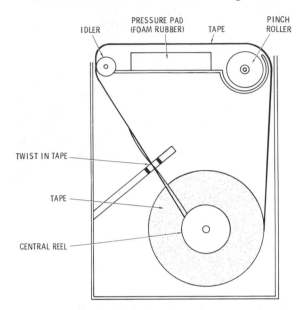

Fig. 9-1. Basic Lear-Jet eight-track cartridge.

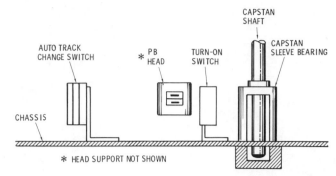

Fig. 9-2. Eight-track player as viewed through the cartridge loading slot.

upwards through a hole cut in the bottom front lip of the four-track cartridge.

Fig. 9-3 shows the motor drive system used in most eight-track machines. The actual position of the flywheel is different on different machines. On some players it will be located beneath the capstan while on others, as in the illustration, it is located above the capstan. One of the purposes of the flywheel is to smooth out minor speed irregularities that can pop up in any mechanical drive system. It also serves to set the gear ratio (for want of a better term) between the capstan and the motor pulley. For correct speed, the important points are the size of the motor pulley, flywheel, and the capstan. Also of prime importance is the speed of the motor and the friction of the drive belt. One major cause of speed variation in these systems is a worn

or dirty belt. It would help reduce the callback rate if every machine serviced would receive a new belt. In any event, the belt should be replaced once a year.

Track Changing

In order to take advantage of all four programs it is necessary to provide a means for varying the height of the playback head relative to the tape surface. This can result in some rather complex mechanical designs for such an apparently simple operation. There are literally dozens of track-change systems in use. Fig. 9-4 shows the Motorola version of one basic type. In Fig. 9-4, the head carriage consists of a molded metal head holder suspended at the end of some metal struts. These struts are anchored in slip-fit holes on a suitable housing. A power spring provides a downward force that tends to keep the head in its lowest position. A transfer pin fitted through a sleeve bearing on the machine chassis provides the upward force needed to vary the height of the head carriage. The position of the transfer pin is determined by the head height cam on which its lower end rides. A

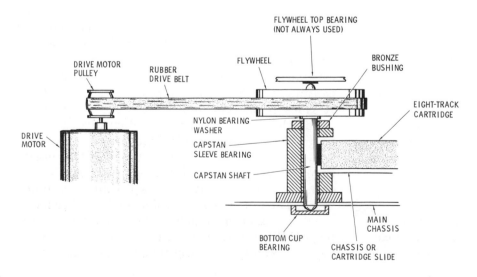

Fig. 9-3. Motor drive system.

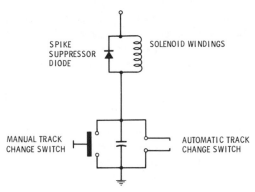

Fig. 9-6. Track-changing circuit.

solenoid, equipped with suitable mechanical linkage, changes the position of the cam in response to commands from either the manual or automatic programing switches. There is always an adjustment in eight-track systems that allows the *fine tuning* of the head height. As mentioned previously, this is very critical if cross talk is to be avoided. Most players will provide a locking nut to fix the position of the adjustment screw once the cross talk is eliminated. This nut must always be tightened after a head alignment. In certain lower-priced models, the adjustment screw must be glued in place after alignment is completed. Most shop glues, or even fingernail polish, are suitable for this purpose.

Fig. 9-5 illustrates the Delco method for setting the head height in the T-400 *Slimline* series players. In this arrangement, the head holder is attached to a flexible nylon parallelogram. This piece is permanently fixed at one end so that as it flexes, the head is moved up and down. A downward force is provided by a leaf spring that presses on top of

the head holder. A post screw is mounted to the head holder. It rests on a head height cam that operates in much the same manner as that of the previous example. There are numerous other methods for varying the head height. Most of them, however, will prove to be a modification of these basic types.

The solenoid that changes the position of the head height cam must be electrically energized each time a track change is desired. In most players, a simple switch (Fig. 9-6) is used for this purpose. Whenever the manual or automatic program switch is closed, current will flow through the solenoid windings, temporarily making it an electromagnet. This causes the plunger to pull inside the coil housing. When the switch is reopened, a power spring on the plunger forces it back to its rest position. A diode is connected across the solenoid windings in order to suppress the high-voltage spike generated by the solenoid inductance when the switch is released. If left unsuppressed, the spike could easily damage the solid-state components in the player.

Another type of track-changing circuit is shown in Fig. 9-7. In this circuit, the two program

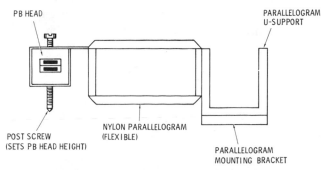

Fig. 9-4. Motorola track-change system.

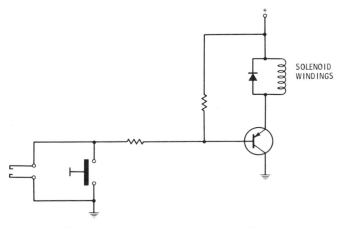

Fig. 9-5. Delco head height adjustment.

Fig. 9-7. Track-changing circuit using a switching transistor.

switches are used to bias a switching transistor. Since the transistor is a pnp, grounding the proper bias resistor will accomplish the switching function. Most of the machines incorporating this type of circuit include a remote jack, so that the program may be changed by a switch located on the car floor close to the driver's left foot. Again, as in the previous circuit example, a diode is used to suppress the high-voltage transient spike generated by the solenoid inductance.

One last, and most unusual, track-changing circuit is the Delco semiconductor controlled rectifier (SCR) system shown in Fig. 9-8. An SCR is a diode rectifier with some very interesting and useful properties. For example, it will not conduct current until after a positive voltage is applied to a third terminal called the *gate*. When the gate voltage is applied, the SCR begins to conduct just like any other diode. The SCR will continue to conduct until the anode-to-cathode current is dropped to a level that is below a certain critical *hold* value. In the Delco circuit, the two program switches are used to supply the gate voltage needed to turn on the SCR. A large forward current will then flow to operate the solenoid. This current is above the value needed to trip the thermal circuit breaker in series with the anode. When the breaker opens— only moments after the initial turn-on, the SCR will turn off. The SCR will remain in the off state after this unless one of the program switches is closed.

There are some unusual complaints generated by this circuit. For example, "my tape player changes programs whenever I operate the power seat (or windows, etc.)." The cause of this symptom is noise spikes entering the player via one of

the lead wires. The cure is to suppress the noise spikes at the offending motor with a suitable bypass (see the chapter on motor noise suppression). In certain severe cases, it may be necessary to replace the motor.

In order to optimize the performance of the eight-track tape player it is necessary to make two basic mechanical adjustments: cross talk and high-frequency response. The *fine tuning* of the head height position is the primary adjustment for eliminating cross talk between programs. This is illustrated in Fig. 9-9. On most machines the adjustment on the head carriage assembly that raises and lowers the head position will be fairly obvious. On some machines, however, it might be wise to consult the appropriate manufacturer's service manual. The usual way to perform this adjustment is to use a prerecorded test tape. The more frequently used test tapes for cross talk alignment feature a silent channel sandwiched between two adjacent channels recorded with constant tones (usually in the 60-125 hertz range). The program selector is set so that the unrecorded track is being played. The head height screw is turned until the tone on the adjacent tracks cannot be heard. In cross talk cases, be sure that the customer's tape is not at fault. Certain defects such as print-through can simulate cross talk most effectively. Cheap tapes exhibit a high degree of cross talk regardless of the head position.

The azimuth of the tape head sets the high-frequency response. For this adjustment it is essential to use an appropriate test tape. A tape recorded with a constant tone in the 6- to 8-kHz region is the usual requirement. Using either an oscilloscope or ac vtvm as an indicator (do not rely on your ears) adjust the azimuth screw for maximum signal level.

Poor high-frequency response can be caused by several defects not related to head alignment. One of these is an excessively worn head. Another, and most frequent defect is excessive tape oxide deposits built up on the surface of the playback head. The cure for the latter defect is a good cleaning with an appropriate head-cleaning solution. It is

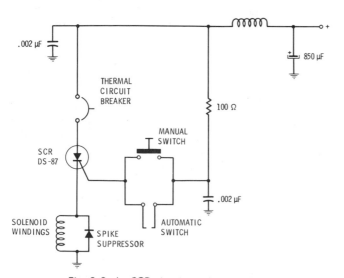

Fig. 9-8. An SCR circuit to change tracks.

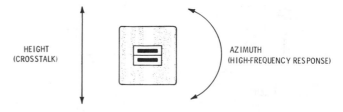

Fig. 9-9. Head movements during alignment.

also a good idea to demagnetize the head. If this is not done, the metal parts that ride on the tape surface will tend to erase the program material beginning with the high frequencies. This can simulate poor frequency response. The defect is, unfortunately, permanent.

Hold/Eject System

Several brands of eight-track tape players use an electromagnet (solenoid) to hold the tape cartridge in place. A flat metal plane attached to the pinch arm interfaces with a flat surface on the front of the electromagnet. When a cartridge is inserted into the machine, a switch is activated that turns on the magnet. There will also be a microswitch operated from the front panel that turns the magnet off when the user wishes to eject the cartridge. Since these switches conduct a high current all the time the player is in use, they have a high failure rate. These switches are a prime suspect when the machine will not hold cartridges. Several imported players used a two-winding solenoid for this function. One was a high-current pull-in winding that had to be turned off almost immediately after the pinch-arm plane was seated. This was accomplished by a small microswitch mounted on the magnet frame. This circuit developed a reputation for blowing fuses. Current practice is to disconnect the microswitch and to connect the two windings in series. Newer replacement solenoids from the various manufacturers delete the high-current winding.

CASSETTE SYSTEM

Fig. 9-10 shows the Philips cassette. This small tape cartridge has found an increasing market in the automotive field. In actuality the cassette is a miniaturized reel-to-reel system. The tape used in cassettes is approximately one-half the size of that used in both eight-track and open-reel machines. At first, the frequency response of the cassette was too poor for good music. Therefore, most earlier cassette players were used primarily for voice recordings. Newer tape formulations and improved players, however, have allowed the cassette to overtake the eight-track format and even approach the performance of some open-reel recorders. The cassette player drive capstan fits through a small hole in the front of the cartridge. This shaft rotates against the pinch roller mounted on the machine. This is illustrated by the drawing in Fig. 9-11. On the rear of the cassette there are two *knock-outs*. These are used to prevent the acci-

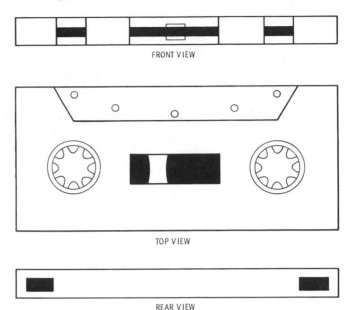

Fig. 9-10. The Philips cassette.

FRONT VIEW

TOP VIEW

REAR VIEW

dental over-recording of prerecorded tape. Machines equipped with the lock-out feature have a small arm that fits into the slot created when the knock-out is removed. When this arm is in the forward position, the record button is rendered inoperative. Blank cassettes come with the knock-outs in place. When the home recordist is satisfied with the material he should remove the knock-out so that his work is not endangered by future recording attempts. Of course, he sacrifices the ability to reuse the cassette for future recording, if he should wish to erase the current material.

Automotive cassette machines are somewhat more flexible than automotive eight-track machines. Few eight-track units, for example, have a fast-forward function. Almost all cassette players have such an ability. The endless loop design of the eight-track cartridge renders a rewind function difficult, if not impossible. Almost every cassette deck allows the user to rewind the tape. The one possible disadvantage to the cassette format for automotive use is that the operator (the driver usually) must perform an operation of some sort to continue listening. He must either rewind the cassette to repeat the same material, eject and flip over the cassette to hear the other side, or eject the cassette and insert another one. The eight-track cartridge will continue playing until the operator shuts it off and removes the tape cartridge.

Drive Mechanisms

Fig. 9-11 shows the diagram of one typical style of cassette drive mechanism. As was true of eight-

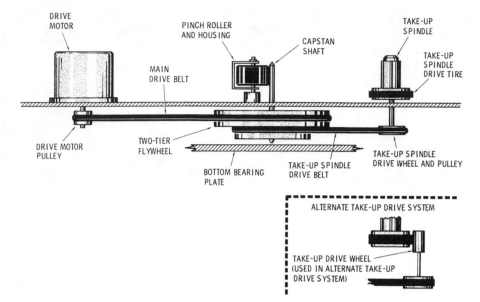

Fig. 9-11. Typical cassette drive mechanism.

track designs, there seems to be an almost endless number of different mechanical designs in the wide range of cassette players available. Limited space does not allow a full discussion of all the many types of mechanisms. The player shown in Fig. 9-11 is in the *play* condition. When the cassette is ejected, the flywheel and related parts will drop down to a rest position so that the cassette can be removed. The drive motor may be found either on the fixed chassis or on the movable chassis. Although both designs are presently in use, most machines mount the motor in the movable chassis to alleviate drive belt stretching problems. The flywheel will be either a two- or three-tier affair in most players. One tier will be directly driven by the motor via a belt. The second tier will be used to drive a take-up pulley. A third tier is occasionally found driving a counter or other function.

The take-up reel can be driven by any one of several alternate methods. The two most common ones are illustrated. The take-up pulley may be driven directly through a clutched shaft, or it may be driven indirectly through a secondary drive wheel.

Fast forward can also be accomplished through several alternate methods. One of the simplest is to use the fast-forward button to remove tension from the pinch roller. This reduces the overall drag and, thereby, speeds up the tape. This system is good from the viewpoint of reliability but its fast-forward speed is not very fast. In other designs, both fast-forward and rewind are accomplished by a pair of drive idlers rotating in opposite directions. These idlers are positioned between the take-up and supply spindles. In the fast-for-

ward mode the pinch roller pressure is removed, and the fast-forward idler is pressed against the take-up spindle drive tire. In this condition, the supply spindle is left free-wheeling (Fig. 9-12). When the machine is shifted into the rewind mode, the opposite idler is used to drive the supply spindle tire, while the take-up spindle free-wheels. In both modes the pinch-roller assembly is moved far enough back to disengage the tape surface and capstan shaft.

Since cassettes do not incorporate an endless loop, it is considered desirable to incorporate an end-of-play automatic ejection system to protect the end anchors inside the cartridges. In order to do this, it is necessary to have a sensor to tell the auto eject circuitry when the tape has finished playing. One such sensor is shown in Fig. 9-13. The sense element is a special wheel attached to the supply spindle. The supply spindle, of course, only turns when the tape is being pulled. When the

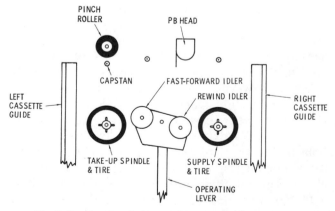

Fig. 9-12. Overhead view of drive system components.

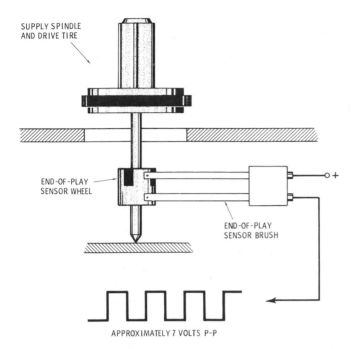

Fig. 9-13. Segmented wheel type end-of-play sensor.

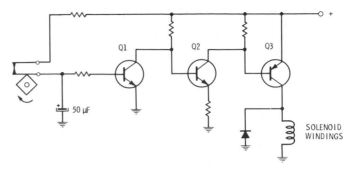

Fig. 9-14. End-of-play eject circuitry.

tape comes to the end of its run, the supply spindle ceases to turn.

The sense wheel consists of two sections. The bottom half is solid copper. The top half has alternate sections of copper and an insulator such as plastic or nylon. The copper sections of the top half are continuous with the copper which makes up the bottom half. A pair of sense brushes rest against this wheel in such a way that one runs on the segmented portion, while the other runs on the solid copper portion. When a dc voltage is applied to one brush, the other will exhibit a square-wave output as long as the sense wheel is turning. When the tape comes to the end of play, the wheel stops. The output from the brush will be either a fixed dc level or it will be zero volts.

There are a number of different sensors in use. Some consist of a spring-wire switch operated by a square cam on the under side of the supply spindle. This mechanism also produces a square-wave output. Still other sensor designs use magnetism to produce the output signal. These systems use a sense wheel (one of two basic types) located between an electromagnet and a pick-up coil. In one common design, the wheel will have alternate sections cut out of its rim so that the magnetic flux is alternately impeded and allowed to flow freely. In another design, there is a brass wheel with the same alternate sections cut out and then refilled with a powdered iron material. The brass impedes the magnetic flux while the powdered iron material

offers it an easier path. The result is a constantly changing magnetic field, as long as the wheel continues to turn. When the wheel stops, the magnetic field will remain at a fixed level, and therefore, no current can be induced into the pick-up coil.

Fig. 9-14 shows one type of end-of-play eject system. When the player is operated, the charging and discharging keeps Q1 saturated. When Q1 is in this condition, the voltage appearing between the collector of Q1 and ground will be close to zero. This causes Q2 and Q3 to cut off. When the tape finishes playing, the charging and discharging will cease. A short time-constant of about eight to twelve seconds keeps Q1 saturated for a time after the tape stops running. When the 50-μF discharges below a certain point, however, Q1 will no longer be forward-biased. This causes Q1 to stop conducting collector current. At this time the voltage between the collector of Q1 and ground rises sufficiently to forward-bias Q2. When Q2 begins conducting, its collector voltage drops. The actual switching transistor (Q3) is directly coupled to the collector of Q2. Therefore, Q3 will go into a conductive state when its base voltage drops relative to its emitter voltage. The collector current that now begins to flow in Q3 is used to energize a solenoid. The plunger of the solenoid is connected to some linkage that disengages the movable platform and allows it to drop out of the way. The power spring that drops the platform is also used to drive the cassette out of its loading slot. When the cassette is first inserted into the slot, there may be a tendency for the eject mechanism to operate too fast. In some players this is overcome by the use of a switch that allows the input hold capacitor to charge rapidly. This switch is usually part of the sense brush assembly.

AUTOMOTIVE TAPE-PLAYER ELECTRONICS

Fig. 9-15 shows the block diagram applicable to most eight-track and cassette electronic sections.

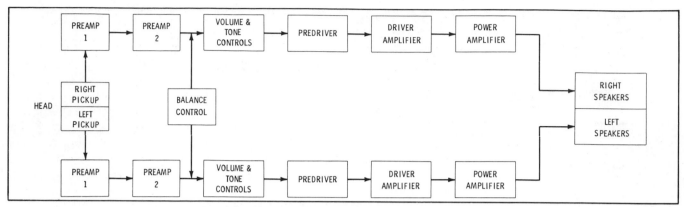

Fig. 9-15. Block diagram of tape player electronic stages.

The playback head feeds a tiny electrical signal to a preamplifier stage. This stage is necessary because the average playback head can deliver only a few millivolts of signal. The output from the preamplifiers is connected to the balance control. This allows the user to set the relative level between the two stereo channels. If this control were not available, it would be necessary to insure that all amplifiers, speakers, and playback heads had virtually identical characteristics and that all listeners be positioned along the line of centers between the two speakers—an impossible situation in an automobile. After the signal passes through the balance control, it is passed through the volume and tone controls. The volume control, of course, sets the level of the sound. The tone controls in most automotive sets are of the treble rolloff variety. Following the control section are the predriver and driver amplifiers. These stages build up the audio signal to a level where it can drive the power amplifier stages. The power amplifiers, of course, drive the speaker systems.

The stages following the control section are too similar to those covered in an earlier chapter to warrant further consideration here. The preamplifiers, however, are specially designed for tape player service. A typical tape preamplifier (transistorized) is shown in Fig. 9-16. It is a simple direct-coupled, two-stage cascade affair. The thing that makes this circuit a tape preamplifier is the fact that the values of the coupling, bypass, and feedback components give the amplifier an NAB tape frequency-response characteristic.

Some of the newer designs are using integrated circuits (ICs) in the tape preamplifier stages. A circuit used by Delco is illustrated in Fig. 9-17. Again, the frequency-response characteristics are suitable for tape. Most IC manufacturers offer what is essentially a dual operational amplifier for

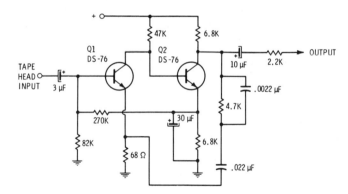

Fig. 9-16. Typical transistorized tape preamplifier.

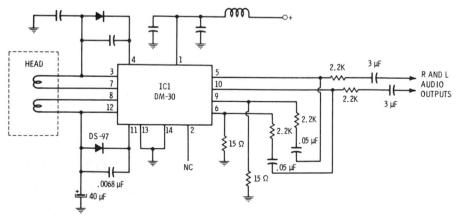

Fig. 9-17. Delco IC tape preamplifier.

stereo preamplifier service. Varying the nature and values of the feedback components will set the overall gain and the shape of the frequency response curve. Lower cost and increased availability make it almost certain that there will be an increase in the number of IC tape preamplifiers.

Very few automotive cassette machines offer a record function; however, the Philips (of Canada) machine used by Chrysler, some of those by Ampex, and certain other imports are excep-

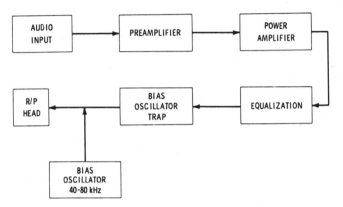

Fig. 9-18. Block diagram of typical record circuits.

tions to the general rule. In almost every case, the record function will follow the block diagram of Fig. 9-18. An audio input is first passed through a preamplifier stage. From there it goes through the regular driver and power amplifier stages. Most of these record stages are also common to the playback mode of operation with a complex switch to select which mode is being used. The signal from the power amplifier is fed to an equalization network that pre-emphasizes the high frequencies. The signal is then applied to the record head along with a constant ac bias signal supplied by an oscillator circuit. This bias signal will have a frequency range usually between 40 and 100 kHz. Its voltage level will be higher than that of the signal being recorded. Because of its high level, it is quite possible for the bias oscillator signal to cause problems in the other stages of the recorder/player. In order to prevent these problems from occuring, there is a parallel-resonant LC trap in the line between the record head and the power amplifier. Although some of the better home machines use an adjustable coil in this trap circuit, most automotive cassette decks use a fixed coil.

Chapter 10

Bench Test Equipment

Vital to the success of any bench service operation is a collection of the proper test equipment. Automotive electronics, fortunately, require only a few of the most basic pieces of electronic test equipment.

POWER SUPPLIES

A source of low-voltage dc power, to simulate the automotive electrical system, is absolutely essential in this type of servicing. The power source that is best suited for any particular shop will, in large measure, depend upon the exact nature of the work being done. For most repair operations on a car radio, a 12-volt dc supply is needed. In the old days some shops used an arrangement such as Fig. 10-1 to generate the necessary voltage and current levels. This system used a generator from a junked automobile. The generator is belt-driven by an ac motor. In modern shops, however, this method is not too feasible.

Another system, also using parts from the automotive electrical system, is shown in Fig. 10-2. This arrangement floats either a battery eliminator or a line-operated charger across an automobile storage battery. A shop that services a large number of the older 6-volt radios can use two series-connected 6-volt batteries each supplied with its own charger. A high-current spdt switch or relay can be used to tap off 6 volts whenever needed. Although this system allows a large current drain for a short period, there are some disadvantages that must not be overlooked. One of these is the danger of overcharging the batteries. Another danger is from acid spills. Battery acid can cause a large amount of damage if it is not properly con-

trolled. Still another danger is the possibility of an explosion, should there be a spark in the vicinity of the cell caps. The explosion is caused by the hydrogen gas generated by the chemical reaction inside each cell. The spark created when disconnecting an operating charger unit is more than enough to make that battery a small but deadly bomb. Another disadvantage, although not a danger, is the necessity of service on a weekly basis. Connections, state of charge, and water levels must be constantly monitored.

The commercial battery eliminator offers the most practical solution to the power problem. The schematic of one popular unit is shown in Fig. 10-3 (Eico model 1064). Whatever supply is chosen, it must have a high degree of filtering so that the audio hum level in the radios will be of little concern. The output voltage should be variable over the range of zero to 20 volts dc.

Another advantageous feature is switch selection of either 6- or 12-volt ranges. The required current capacity will depend mostly on the type of service work expected. If only tape player and simple car radio service is contemplated, the supply must be capable of providing approximately 5 amperes at 14.4-volts dc output. If you plan to service *Wonder Bar* (Delco) or other solenoid type signal-seeker radios, the supply must be able to offer 16 amperes without losing regulation (E-out must be greater than 12 volts dc) for a short period of time. The Eico 1064 and those supplies offered by the Delco Electronics Division of General Motors have found a measure of popularity in car radio shops. There are, however, many very suitable supplies offered by an almost endless list of manufacturers. Some supplies are even better suited to

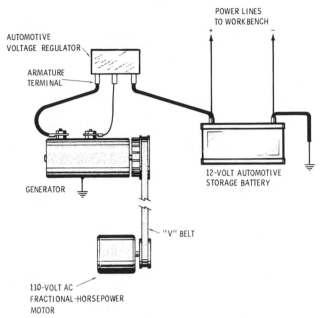

Fig. 10-1. Old-style bench power system.

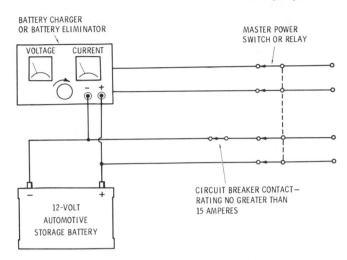

Fig. 10-2. Bench power system with a battery charger.

this type of duty than are the most popular numbers.

METERS

The service bench should be supplied with a good quality vtvm or FETVM. The requirements for service-grade meters are equally valid in the car radio/tape-player shop. Since all modern car radios are solid-state, it is wise to choose a meter with a very low range. Meters that allow a full-scale deflection with an input of 1 V dc or less are highly desirable. Since germanium transistors operate at a forward-bias of .2 volt, the author prefers those meters that offer the popular .5-1.5-5-15 volt sequence of dc scales.

A small, portable vom is handy for use in automobiles. These meters see a lot of rugged use, so choose one of reasonably tough construction. A sensitivity rating of 1000 ohms-per-volt is fine for an in-the-car meter, but not for bench use. Surpris-

ingly, the small, inexpensive voms seem to hold up better bouncing around than some of the more expensive meters. In a pinch, intelligent use of a 12-volt pilot lamp, mounted in a holder for protection and connected to a pair of alligator clip leads, will do almost as good a job as a meter.

Shops doing a lot of tape player work will be able to use a good service or lab-grade ac vtvm. An example of such a meter is shown in Fig. 10-5. These meters can be valuable in testing tape playback heads prior to replacement. It will allow making a decision concerning the condition of the head without resorting to the substitution method.

SIGNAL GENERATORS

There are several styles of signal generators needed in automotive electronics. Perhaps the most basic of these is the service-grade rf signal generator (Fig. 10-6). It is not necessary to spend the large sums required to obtain a lab-grade instrument for use in a-m radio servicing. The particular generator chosen should cover the frequency range of 200 kHz to 11.0 MHz or more. This will allow the complete alignment of an a-m radio and the i-f

Fig. 10-3. Schematic of the Eico battery eliminator.

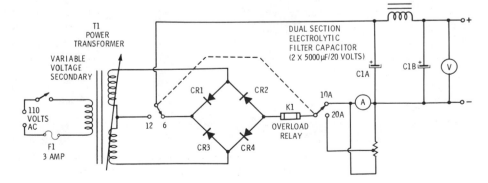

alignment of fm sets. Reasonably good shielding is a must. It is very difficult to properly align a radio if more rf escapes around the cabinet flanges of the generator than comes through the output jack. Desirable features include an attenuator, a modulation switch with either "off" or "external" positions, and an output level meter. Of these, the output meter can be considered optional. Reasonable stability is also demanded. It cannot be tolerated if the generator changes frequency by an appreciable amount during the short time required for radio alignment.

An audio generator producing both sine and square waves is also of use. Two examples of this type of instrument are shown, one in Fig. 10-7 and the other in Fig. 10-8. The output level of the audio generator should be variable from zero to at least .1 volt rms. Although the uses for a sine-wave generator can be easily appreciated, there might be some question about the use of the square-wave function. The reason for using the square-wave

generator is the rather impressive frequency response specifications found on some modern automotive electronics equipment. Stereo fm is capable of a 15-kHz frequency response, while tape players can offer up to at least 12 kHz. In the near future, tape improvements may bring this medium at least up to the level of fm stereo. The ease of making quick frequency response checks with a square wave makes this style of generator increasingly useful.

There is available a type of "quickie" signal generator that proves very useful in troubleshooting a-m radios and tape players. These generators are housed in a "penlight" flashlight case. They are generally little more than a transistor square-wave generator operating in the 1000-Hz range. The harmonics of these generators will extend, with usable strength, all the way up to some frequency range above the a-m broadcast band. The low price of these portable noise generators can

Courtesy EICO

Fig. 10-4. Battery eliminator.

Courtesy EICO

Fig. 10-5 Eico ac vtvm.

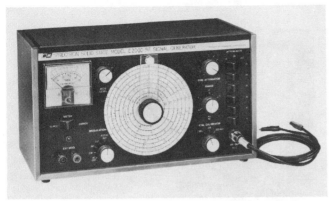

Courtesy Dynascan Corp.

Fig. 10-6. An rf signal generator.

easily justify the purchase. In a pinch, however, the bench square-wave generator can be pressed into the same use with acceptable results.

On most older fm car radios the alignment can be performed with the low-cost service-grade rf signal generator. In more modern sets, however, performance levels are such that a lab-grade fm signal generator is almost mandatory. These generators, unfortunately, are very expensive. It is possible, however, to obtain such instruments at a more reasonable price on the used market or through firms that handle large amounts of government and industrial surplus electronics equipment. There are a number of firms that advertise either rebuilt or as-is lab-grade instruments. Consult the advertising in the various trade magazines.

Since a large number of American car radios are equipped for fm stereo reception, it is mandatory for the service technician to have an fm stereo generator or simulator for troubleshooting and alignment of the stereo decoder sections of the receivers. There are several generators available in

Courtesy EICO

Fig. 10-8. Eico FET sine/square-wave generator.

kit form. One of these generators is shown in Fig. 10-9. One feature the author considers vital is crystal control of the 19,000-Hz pilot signal. Beyond that, most of the various features tend to be a matter of preference or convenience rather than dire necessity. Although these generators are nominally priced they are by no means undesirable for use in a car radio shop.

MISCELLANEOUS INSTRUMENTS

There is one low-cost test instrument that is almost an absolute necessity to a car radio troubleshooter: the signal tracer. This instrument is basically little more than a high-gain audio amplifier with a speaker output. To be useful in the non-

Courtesy Dynascan Corp.

Fig. 10-7. Precision sine/square-wave generator.

Courtesy Heath Co.

Fig. 10-9. Heath fm stereo generator.

audio stages of the radio (rf, i-f, and converter), the signal tracer should be equipped with either a demodulator probe or an internal switch selected demodulator circuit. Most signal tracers also include accessory jacks to facilitate the testing of speakers and audio output transformers by the substitution method. An example of a modern solid-state signal tracer is shown in Fig. 10-10.

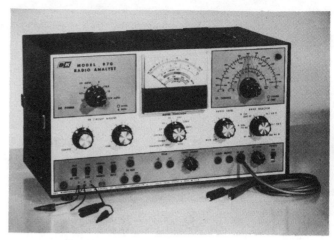

Courtesy Dynascan Corp.

Fig. 10-11. A radio analyst.

A cheaper way to check tape-player speed involves the use of specially prepared test tapes. Most of the appropriate tapes have a continuous 60-Hz tone recorded on one track. This tone is punctuated every 59 seconds by a 1000-Hz tone burst of one second duration. A watch with a sweep second hand or a stop watch is used to measure the time interval between tone bursts. Most tape player manufacturers, at least in the automotive market, allow a plus or minus three-second tolerance for such tests. The 60-Hz tone can also be used for speed tests if it is accurate. This test in-

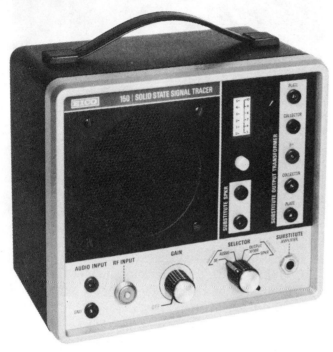

Courtesy EICO

Fig. 10-10. Solid-state signal tracer.

The digital frequency counter (DFC) was once the type of instrument found only where money was no object. Heath and others, however, have changed that situation by offering, either ready-built or in kit form, DFCs with low price tags and impressive specifications. These instruments offer a lot of convenience on an automotive electronics service bench. Some cassette player manufacturers are currently recommending the use of a DFC, in conjunction with a standard test tape, to check or set the variable speed controls in their respective machines. The DFC is also useful in checking the operation of the local oscillator in an a-m car radio. With an appropriate scaler they can also be used with fm radios. Another use is the calibration of shop signal generators. Most shop-grade signal generators are not particularly accurate in the vicinity of the 10.7-MHz fm i-f frequency. As more of these instruments find their way into service ships, it is certain that they will play an ever-expanding role in our daily work.

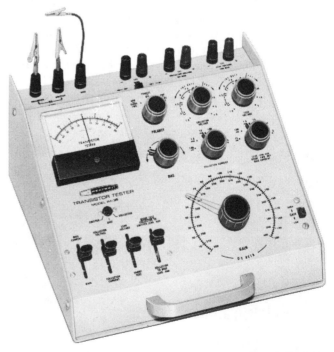

Courtesy Heath Co.

Fig. 10-12 Out-of-circuit transistor tester.

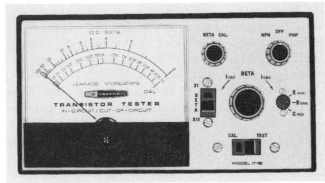

Courtesy Heath Co.

Fig. 10-13. In-circuit transistor tester.

volves using an oscilloscope set to synchronize the horizontal sweep to the 60-Hz ac power line. (On most oscilloscopes all that is necessary is to set the horizontal sweep and sync controls to "line.") When the output from the tape player is connected to the vertical amplifier, the screen will show an almost circular Lissajous pattern. Adjust the tape-player speed control until the pattern locks and ceases rotation. Most test tapes also offer a 7- or 8-kHz tone for head azimuth alignment and a cross-talk check for the head height alignment. The

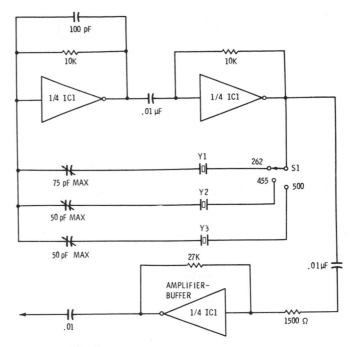

IC1: RTL QUAD TWO-INPUT GATE
Y1: 262.5-kHz PARALLEL-RESONANT CRYSTAL
Y2: 455-kHz PARALLEL-RESONANT CRYSTAL
Y3: 500-kHz PARALLEL-RESONANT CRYSTAL

Fig. 10-14. Schematic of integrated-circuit crystal calibrator.

Fig. 10-15. Two schematics of crystal calibrators usable for alignment of fm car radios.

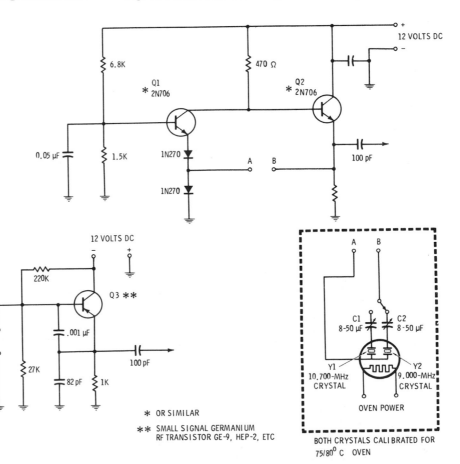

* OR SIMILAR

** SMALL SIGNAL GERMANIUM RF TRANSISTOR GE-9, HEP-2, ETC

BOTH CRYSTALS CALIBRATED FOR 75/80° C OVEN

latter test usually consists of a low-frequency tone on one of the center tracks with the two adjacent tracks silent. The player indexing is set to one of the silent tracks. If any tone is heard, the head height adjustment is turned until the unwanted tone is nulled completely out.

Wow and flutter are forms of low-frequency fm modulation to a recorded tone due to speed variations in the playback machine. A wow and flutter meter measures this modulation and expresses the result as a percentage figure. Although these meters can prove handy in the servicing of automotive tape players, they are currently too costly to be considered any more than a luxury. Since most eight-track and cassette playback machines made for the automotive market have high levels of wow and flutter to begin with, little improvement can be expected by the use of an expensive wow and flutter meter. In the future, however, machines can be expected to improve to a point that makes the investment more attractive. It is even possible that an increased market for such devices will spur competition among manufacturers, resulting in a reduction of average price levels.

From time to time, a manufacturer comes out with an instrument of unique flexibility. Such an instrument is the radio analyst shown in Fig. 10-11. This instrument combines in one cabinet the basic functions of several popular and useful service instruments. The price of the analyst is nominal compared to the total cost of the equivalent instruments purchased separately.

Since all modern car radios are solid-state, it is advisable for the technician to have a decent transistor tester. Two suitable transistor testers are illustrated in Figs. 10-12 and 10-13. The first type is an out-of-circuit instrument. The other, although less flexible, is for in-circuit use. The author leans heavily toward the out-of-circuit type because they tend to be more accurate. Since these instruments are in a reasonable price range, it is not uncommon to find shops that use both types to best advantage.

Crystal calibrators serve several useful functions in any service operation. They can be used for troubleshooting, as marker generators during alignment, and for the calibration of test equipment. Three useful types are shown in Figs. 10-14, 10-15, and 10-16. The type in Fig. 10-14 is used to align a-m radio receivers. It has three crystal-controlled frequencies: 262 kHz, 455 kHz, and 500 kHz. The 262-kHz frequency is used to align the standard American car radio i-f amplifier. The 455-kHz crystal is used to align the standard

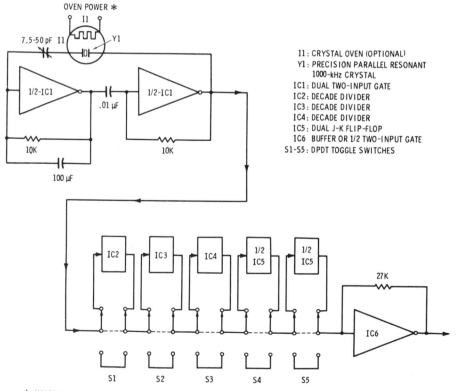

I1: CRYSTAL OVEN (OPTIONAL)
Y1: PRECISION PARALLEL RESONANT 1000-kHz CRYSTAL
IC1: DUAL TWO-INPUT GATE
IC2: DECADE DIVIDER
IC3: DECADE DIVIDER
IC4: DECADE DIVIDER
IC5: DUAL J-K FLIP-FLOP
IC6 BUFFER OR 1/2 TWO-INPUT GATE
S1-S5: DPDT TOGGLE SWITCHES

* VOLTAGE AND CURRENT RATING DEPENDENT UPON PARTICULAR OVEN BEING USED

Fig. 10-16. Universal crystal calibrator.

American home radio i-f and some European car radio i-f amplifiers. The 500-kHz frequency is used to set local oscillator tracking in the front-end of the radio. Although some radios will tune down to 500 kHz on the low end of the dial, it is the second and third harmonics that are of primary interest. These harmonics fall at 1000 and 1500 kHz, two useful points to check a-m radio dial tracking.

Fig. 10-15 shows a crystal oscillator used to align fm car radios. This circuit was adapted from a similar design found in the Editors & Engineers book titled *The Radio Handbook.* It is advisable to follow either of these circuits with a buffer amplifier to reduce frequency pulling caused by changing load conditions. The choice of the 10.7-MHz crystal is obvious since this is the standard fm i-f in American-made radios. The 9-MHz crystal, however, requires a bit of explanation. Harmonics of 9 MHz fall at convenient points in the fm band: 90, 99, and 108 MHz. These are nearly ideal for checking the front-end dial tracking. Tracking checks are made by setting the radio dial to one of these frequencies and then adjusting the local oscillator trimmer in the radio until the generator signal falls in the middle of the radio passband. You can monitor the afc correction voltage on most

sets to determine when the middle of the passband has been reached. The afc voltage will be either positive or negative, depending upon whether the local oscillator is tracking above or below the correct frequency. When the local oscillator is on the correct frequency, the afc correction voltage will be zero.

The circuit shown in Fig. 10-16 is a universal crystal calibrator that has a wide range of uses. Most of these have to do with the calibration of shop test equipment. The IC dividers reduce the frequency of the 1-MHz source by a factor of either 10 or 2, depending upon which is being used. With this arrangement, you can generate very accurate and stable frequencies at 1 MHz, 500 kHz, 250 kHz, 100 kHz, 50 kHz, 25 kHz, 10 kHz, 5 kHz, and 2.5 kHz. For maximum accuracy the trimmer capacitor can be used to zero beat the source oscillator against the National Bureau of Standards radio station WWV. In Figs. 10-14 and 10-15 the use of the crystal oven is a desirable option. In the high-accuracy calibrator of Fig. 10-16, however, it must be considered necessary. These ovens can be purchased for usually less than 20 dollars, and many surplus dealers offer ex-military and commercial ovens for much less.

Chapter 11

Car Radio Troubleshooting

For most service technicians the first encounter with a defective car radio will be while it is still installed in a vehicle. Since removal can be difficult in many cases, all possible information pertaining to the defect should be found. This information is obtained through the use of certain preliminary checks.

PRELIMINARY TESTING

Most car radios using solid-state output stages will produce a *thump* in the speaker whenever power is applied or removed. This is characteristic of single-ended output circuits. Push-pull circuits, fortunately in the minority, do not usually produce this effect. Assuming that the radio is not working the presence of this thumping sound is an indication that the speaker is good. Should there be no thump, try placing your ear close to the radio chassis (if possible) while tuning across the band. The laminations in the output transformer or choke coil will vibrate in step with the applied signal causing the familiar *transformer talk*. This is a good indication that the trouble is either in the speaker or in the connections between the radio chassis and the speaker. A substitute speaker will tell the final story.

If, on the other hand, there is speaker thump, you can forget about the speaker temporarily. It will be necessary to uncover through other means the defect that is causing the malfunction. However, after that problem is cured you recheck the speaker for fidelity. The next step will be to turn the volume control shaft through its range several times. If you hear a slight scratching sound, it is very probable that the defect is prior to the audio-amplifier section. The scratching is caused by dirt on the volume control wiper and element. If it is audible, you can be reasonably sure that the audio amplifiers have plenty of gain. This subjective test does not, by the way, exonerate the audio amplifiers in cases of distortion. The last subjective test to make is to turn the volume control to full loudness. If there is a high hiss level, the car antenna should be suspect. This hiss is caused by each amplifying stage in the radio and by the mixer action. If all stages are amplifying, this background hiss becomes quite loud. The most probable defects in such a case are a bad antenna or transmission line, a defective rf amplifier in the radio, or a converter stage that is still amplifying but not oscillating. A test antenna should be tried on the radio in these situations prior to removal from the car. Most shops keep a test antenna (a low cost *eight ball* is fine) and a test speaker handy in the radio removal work area, so that unnecessary removals can be avoided if possible.

The power source is often a cause of trouble in automotive electronic equipment. The most obvious and frequent occurrence is an open fuse. A good rule of thumb to remember is that fuses do not cause trouble; they indicate trouble. Although *you* know this is true, your customer may tend to disagree. Be aware, however, that in many modern cars one fuse *protects* many circuits. If there is a 9-ampere fuse serving a radio that requires a maximum of 1.2 amperes, you may have a defect elsewhere. A common problem in some cars is the case where the radio fuse also serves either the backup lamps or the brake lamps of the car. You may replace a fuse in the radio, but when the customer puts his car in reverse to back out of your shop a defective backup circuit causes the fuse to blow again.

One other power source defect that is seen relatively often is a reversed battery polarity. Fig. 11-1 shows a pair of simple polarity checkers that can be used to spot these defects. The model illustrated in Fig. 11-1B uses two lamps. One of these will light up if the battery is connected negative to ground while the other will light up if the battery is positively grounded. On late model American-made cars and on most foreign-made cars the battery should be installed with the negative terminal to ground. Unfortunately, careless service station attendants will often install a new or recharged battery backwards. A reversed-polarity battery can fool almost anything on the car. The exceptions are those items that contain solid-state electronic components. Transistor car radios will blow the output transistor when exposed to reversed polarity. Also endangered are the electrolytic decoupling capacitors in the power supply. These days the damage resulting from a reversed battery will cost the owner less than twenty dollars. In the future, electronics will play an increasing role in automotive designs; sloppy battery installation in cars of the future could easily wipe out the radio, the fuel injection computer, temperature regulation computer, solid-state voltage regulator, automatic dimmer amplifier and sensors, etc.

Once it has been determined that the problem is inside the radio rather than in one of the other accessories attached to the radio, it will be necessary to remove the radio chassis from the car. The test equipment needed for car radio service work is limited. A previous chapter gives details concerning this type of equipment required. If a full-time car radio man is employed, it might be wise to

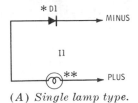

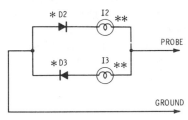

(A) Single lamp type.

(B) Double lamp type.

Fig. 11-1. Simple polarity checkers.

custom-build his workbench in order to improve the overall efficiency. A good installation will include two permanently mounted eight ball antennas, four speakers mounted in the bench, and a power source capable of running two fm stereo radios or one signal seeker. If this bench is to be used to service a large quantity of relatively few models, then you could also make wiring harnesses that would allow these models to be connected quickly. The author keeps harness permanently wired for General Motors, Ford Motor Company, and Chrysler Corporation radios.

DC CIRCUIT ANALYSIS

The radio to be considered here is the typical a-m band car radio. A block diagram of such a receiver is shown in Fig. 11-2. If the previously men-

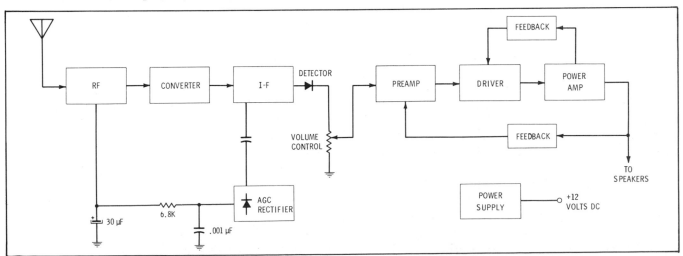

Fig. 11-2. Block diagram of a typical a-m superhet radio.

tioned scratching from the volume control is audible, then you may safely assume that the trouble is in the front end of the radio. The first consideration in troubleshooting in a front-end problem is the action of the agc voltage. This voltage will appear at the collector of an rf amplifier using pnp transistors and at the emitter of an rf amplifier using npn transistors. In both cases, the level of the agc voltage should rise and fall as the set is tuned across stations. If the agc voltage does vary in this manner, you may eliminate the rf amplifier, the converter, and the input half of the i-f amplifier as the defective stages. In this particular situation, the trouble will most likely be found in the circuits that are between the agc takeoff point (collector of the i-f transistor) and the input to the volume control.

If the agc voltage does not vary as the radio is tuned, you must look for a defect between the antenna and the agc takeoff point. The next step in this case is to make dc conduction checks in the three front-end stages. This is illustrated in Fig. 11-3 and 11-4. If the radio uses npn transistors, use the procedure detailed in Fig. 11-3. Connect the minus lead of the vtvm to chassis ground. Touch the positive probe of the vtvm to the emitter terminal of each transistor in succession. Although the expected voltages will vary from set to set, those shown in the illustration are typical. If the radio uses pnp transistors in the front end, use the procedure of Fig. 11-4. Reverse the leads or set the vtvm to the dc-minus function. Connect the common lead of the vtvm to the B+ line that serves the rf, converter, and i-f stages. Connect the probe of the vtvm to each emitter in succession. The voltage levels shown in this diagram are also fairly typical. A defect will usually show up as a wide variation from the normal. If a transistor is

open, for example, there will be zero volts on the emitter. If, on the other hand, the transistor is either shorted or extremely leaky, the conduction voltage drop will be excessive. A shorted transistor could easily allow the full terminal voltage to appear across the emitter resistor. Conduction current can be helpful information. By Ohm's law, we can state that conduction current approximates:

$$I_E = \frac{E_{ER}}{R_E}$$

where,
    I_E is the emitter current in amperes,
    E_{ER} is the emitter resistor voltage drop in volts,
    R_E is the resistance of emitter resistor in ohms.

In most car radio receivers, the conduction current of the three front-end stages will be between .75 and 2.0 milliamperes.

Next, a dc check of transistor biasing is needed. The exact value of a particular bias voltage is determined primarily by the type of material from which the transistor is made. Germanium transistors will have a forward bias close to .2 V dc, while silicon transistors will exhibit a forward-bias near .6 V dc. Fig. 11-5 shows two typical transistors and the relative voltages that will be found. Any large departure from these normals should be investigated. An analysis of bias and conduction voltages can often lead to an indication of exactly what is wrong with a transistor. A high bias voltage across the base-emitter junction as well as zero transistor conduction, indicates an open emitter. A normal forward-bias voltage with

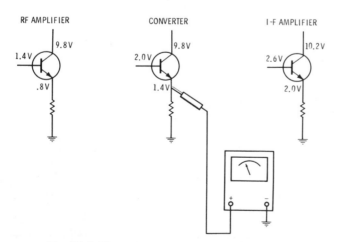

Fig. 11-3. Checking dc conduction in npn stages.

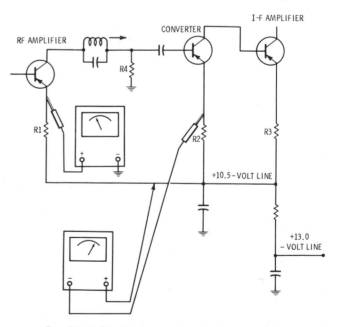

Fig. 11-4. Checking dc conduction in pnp stages.

COLLECTOR

BASE

E_B

EMITTER

PNP

COLLECTOR

BASE

E_B

EMITTER

NPN

BIAS VALUES (E_B): GERMANIUM TRANSISTORS = .2 VOLT DC
SILICON TRANSISTORS = .6 VOLT DC

Fig. 11-5. Bias checks for npn and pnp transistors.

zero transistor conduction means a probable open collector. Zero forward bias with either zero or very high (abnormal) conduction indicates a shorted base-emitter junction.

AC CIRCUIT ANALYSIS

Unfortunately not all defects manifest themselves as changes in dc levels. In those cases where an analysis of dc conditions is insufficient, it might be necessary to resort to signal injection and signal-tracing methods. The signal-tracing method is illustrated in Fig. 11-6. In this method, you connect a signal source to the antenna circuit. This source can be either a signal generator or a broadcast station signal. In either situation, you use the tracer to look for the signal at several key points in the radio. The signal should be found at the collector of the rf amplifier, the base of the converter, the collector of the converter, the base of the i-f amplifier, the collector of the i-f amplifier, and on both sides of the diode detector. At some point in this

chain, you should lose the signal. The defect will be found between that point and the last point where the signal level was normal.

The alternate system for isolating a defective stage is called signal injection. This is illustrated in Fig. 11-7. In this system, keep an output monitor connected to the speaker line of the radio. In most cases, the speaker itself will serve admirably as the output indicator. The output of an appropriate signal generator is injected into the input of each stage in succession, until a point is found where no signal will pass. An audio generator must be used in the circuits after the detector and an rf generator prior to the detector. It is mandatory that the level of the signal generator be kept only high enough to produce a usable output. If the level is extreme, it can easily shock-excite defective parts into temporary operation.

Spurious oscillations in one stage or another will be encountered in any type of radio service. These oscillations will fall into one of two catagories: tunable and nontunable. The nontunable types will remain constant as the radio dial is tuned. Such oscillations include motorboating and whistling. These conditions are almost always created in the audio stages, a fact that accounts for their being nontunable.

Tunable oscillations occur in one of the three front-end stages. They are most frequently caused by defects in the agc loop. A tunable oscillation will vary in pitch as the radio is tuned across a station. As the station is tuned in, the pitch of the oscillation will drop to zero (zero beat) when the radio

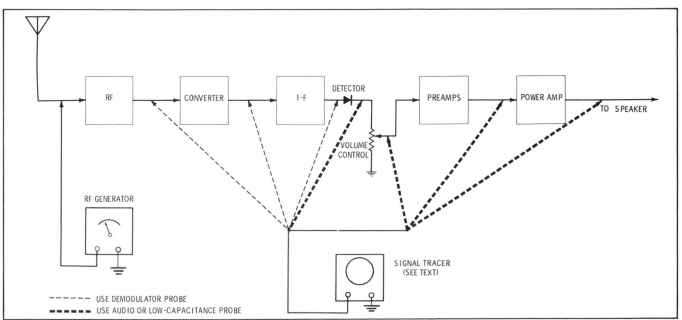

Fig. 11-6. Signal tracing technique for stage isolation.

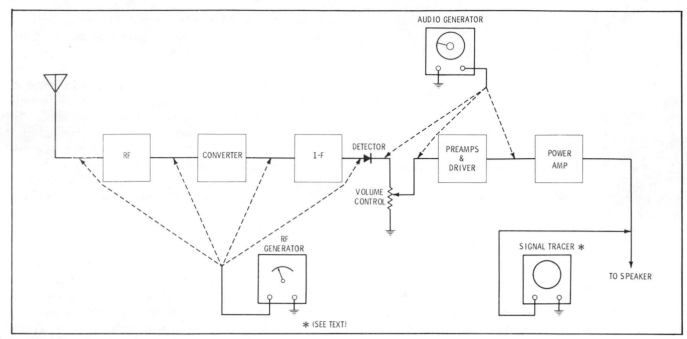

Fig. 11-7. Signal injection technique for stage isolation.

is tuned directly on the center of the station signal. As the dial is moved past the station, the pitch of the oscillation will rise until it is beyond human hearing. Also, agc loop oscillation is often accompanied by agc distortion. In these cases the radio will distort badly on strong stations but may play normally on weaker stations. Look first for an open electrolytic agc bypass capacitor or an open agc rectifier diode. In older radios using germanium transistors, a similar set of symptoms could appear if excessive base-to-collector leakage occurred in any of the transistors. This problem could occur in any of the front-end transistors.

AUDIO STAGES

In the old days, audio stages were isolated from each other by either transformer or RC coupling. All modern car radios, however, use a cascade direct-coupled type of circuit. In these circuits, a defect anywhere in the three audio stages could affect the operation of and dc voltage readings in any and all remaining stages.

It is the conduction of the output transistor that tells the story in audio-section troubleshooting. Figs. 11-8 and 11-9 show where the output transistor conduction voltages are to be measured. In Fig. 11-8 you see the usual output configuration for negative ground radios using a pnp power transistor. The dc voltage appearing between the collector of this transistor and ground is the key to circuit operation. In most car radios, this volt-

age will be in the neighborhood of .6 to 2.0 V dc. Since there is such a wide variation, it would be wise to consult the service literature for each model to find the precise value.

Testing Output Transistors

In Fig. 11-9, a conduction check is used on a radio with an npn output transistor. In this type of circuit, it is the voltage appearing between the emitter and ground that is important. It will generally have a level of 2.0 to 3.0 V dc. A high voltage at this point could mean either a shorted transistor or an open circuit between the emitter and ground. A good determining indicator may be found by monitoring the primary current drain of the radio. Most service-type power supplies include an ammeter for this purpose. If the meter shows a heavy current flow, the transistor must be assumed to be shorted. If, on the other hand, the

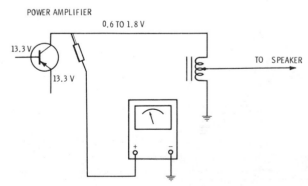

Fig. 11-8. Checking the conduction of a pnp output stage.

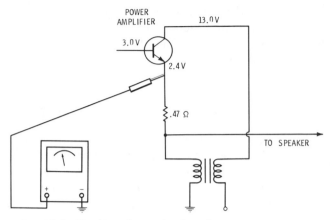

Fig. 11-9. Checking the conduction of an npn output stage.

drain is only a few milliamperes, the defect will probably be an open fuse resistor or transformer winding.

Fig. 11-10 shows a typical car radio audio output stage using a pnp power transistor. Being directly coupled, any defects in any stage can and will affect the output transistor stage. The following discussion will consider the trouble-shooting procedure for two symptoms, both of which result in a dead output stage. In the first, the output transistor will be cut off, while in the second, the output transistor will appear shorted.

First, however, let's quickly review the operation of this type of circuit. The conduction of the power transistor Q3 is increased by a decrease in the voltage appearing between its base terminal and ground. This voltage can be decreased by heavily forward-biasing the driver transistor Q2. The conduction of Q2 is increased by increasing its base to ground voltage. This can be accomplished by turning off the preamplifier transistor Q1. Conduction in Q3 increases, as the conduction in Q2 increases and while the conduction of Q1 decreases. The exact opposite must occur if the conduction of Q3 is to be decreased.

Assume that you have a radio in which the power transistor Q3 appears to be either saturated or shorted. The first step will be to short together the base and emitter terminals of Q3 while monitoring the collector voltage. If the meter reading drops considerably when the base and emitter terminals are shorted, you can be reasonably sure that the transistor is working. This test shows that the base is capable of controlling collector current.

If the power transistor proves to be working, it will be necessary to consider next the driver transistor as a possible source of trouble. This can be determined by shorting together the Q2 base and

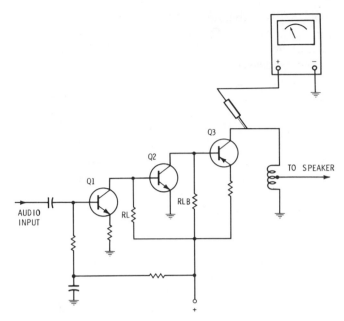

Fig. 11-10. Typical car radio audio output stage.

emitter terminals. If Q2 is operating properly, this test should cause the power transistor Q3 to cut off. If Q2 is shorted, the test will not affect the conduction of Q3. Also, Q3 will appear shorted if the preamplifier transistor Q1 ceases to conduct.

It is also helpful on some occasions to make dc voltage readings on Q1. In certain Delco radios made during the mid-sixties the Q1 emitter resistor was actually a bias potentiometer. These pots had a habit of becoming an open circuit. When this occurred, both the emitter voltage of Q1 and the collector voltage of Q3 would shoot up to an abnormally high level. The cure, of course, was a new bias pot.

In certain other radios you may see a symptom where Q3 appears to be cut off. In this instance the first step is to determine whether or not the output transistor is working. One quick way to make this determination in the circuit is to shunt a resistor between the base of Q3 and ground. The value of this resistor should be less than 220 ohms at 1 watt. If the power transistor is good, the collector voltage will rise when the resistor is connected. Should the power transistor be good, you must look at other stages to find the fault. If the driver transistor Q2 is cut off, you can also expect to find Q3 cut off. Step two would be to attempt to turn on Q2 by bridging a 100,000-ohm resistor between the collector and the base. If Q2 is good, you should see an increase in the Q3 collector voltage while the resistor is in the circuit. If the transistor Q1 is shorted, the output transistor will cut off. A short in Q1 will cause its collector voltage to drop drastically. Although shorting the base and emitter terminals of Q1 will tell us if it is good, this operation is not recommended. Cutting off Q1 will cause excessive current to flow in Q3; this current may damage Q3 and the output transformer. It is recommended that these transistors be checked out of the circuit after a dc voltage analysis leads you to suspect that the transistor is at fault.

Transistors can be quick-checked with an ohmmeter. Measure small signal transistors on the R×100 scale and power transistors on either the R×10 or R×1 scale according to their size. Be absolutely sure of the type battery used in your ohmmeter. It must not be any larger than 1.5 volts. Older ohmmeters that used a 22.5-volt battery are not suitable for transistor testing. This type of test depends upon the ohmmeter to turn on the transistor junctions. Certain newer FET meters use a .1 V dc or less source for the ohmmeter. This, in effect, renders the ohmmeter useless as a transistor tester.

The procedure for testing transistors with a conventional 1.5-volt ohmmeter is simple. Measure the resistance between the base and collector terminals. Then reverse the ohmmeter probes and again make the same measurement. One of the two readings should be considerably higher than the other. In fact, the higher reading should be at least ten times the lower reading. The base-emitter juncction is checked in the same manner. It is important that you remain on the same ohmmeter scale throughout this test. Different scales will place different voltage levels across the measured junction. This, in effect, renders the test meaningless.

The ohmmeter can also be used to determine whether or not the base is capable of controlling the collector current. For this test you must know the dc polarity of the ohmmeter. In most instruments the positive pole of the battery will be connected to the positive probe. For pnp transistors, connect the negative terminal of the ohmmeter to the collector. If the transistor is an npn type, connect the positive terminal of the ohmmeter to the collector. The emitter of the transistor should be connected to the remaining ohmmeter lead. The test is carried out by touching the base to the collector. This should cause the meter reading to drop considerably. If the meter shows low resistance with the base open or if it fails to show a drop in resistance when the base is connected to the collector, then consider the transistor as bad. Care must be exercised in this type of testing so that the transistor will not be destroyed by excessive current flow. Always use one of the low-current ranges of the ohmmeter. This means R×100 or higher. Also, never perform this test in the circuit with power applied. Under such circumstances transistor damage is certain.

SOLVING INTERMITTENT TROUBLES

The extreme environmental conditions under which auto electronic equipment must perform cause a large amount of intermittent trouble. These conditions can be caused by vibration, by too much heat, or by letting the radio get too cold. Vibration-sensitive defects can be found in most instances by tapping the printed-circuit board with a lightweight insulated tool such as the handle of a small screw driver. Heat problems can often be located by touching suspected parts with either a soldering iron or a small light bulb. Cases of stage isolation can be handled by allowing the radio to operate under a heat lamp, until the failure is generated. Radios that fail to play when cold can present a bit of a problem. Parts that are suspected can be cooled off by the use of one of the Freon aerosols used for this purpose. These sprays are, however, rather expensive to use in stage isolation. If the radio is stored in the shop refrigerator over night, you can expect about 20 minutes of troubleshooting time in the morning. Even if the precise part that is defective is not located you should at least be able to isolate the defective stage in that time. The few remaining components can be examined with the freeze spray until the bad one is located.

THE CONVERTER

The converter stage in a car radio can be rather troublesome to service. In this stage, the dc condition is frequently found to be in good order, yet the set will still fail to operate. The converter stage is a combination circuit which performs the functions of both the mixer and the local oscillator. If the local oscillator function of the converter fails, it is still possible for the stage to amplify. The result is a high hiss level that sounds much like the hiss present when the rf amplifier is defective. When this is the problem, it is necessary to determine whether the oscillator is actually running and at what frequency. The usual method for checking the oscillator involves measuring the dc conduction while tuning the radio all the way across the band. Since the stage is more efficient at one end or the other, the result of this test will be a converter conduction voltage that varies as the radio is tuned. A constant voltage means that the oscillator is not oscillating. Unfortunately, this test will only tell us whether or not the oscillator is oscillating; it will not tell us whether or not the frequency is correct.

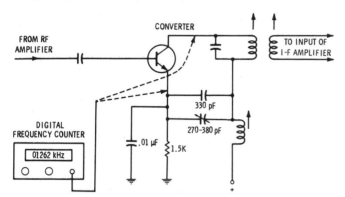

Fig. 11-11. Using the DFC to troubleshoot a converter.

The availability of low-cost digital frequency counters (DFCs) allows us to troubleshoot converter stages more effectively. The DFC actually counts the number of cycles that pass through its input gate during a given time period. It then displays this information as a function of events per unit of time. Fig. 11-11 shows the two points in a typical converter stage where DFC readings can be taken. In most cases the emitter of the transistor will be the point of choice, because there are no errors due to modulation frequencies present here. In certain types of radios, however, the voltage generated at this point will not be sufficient to drive your counters. In this instance use the collector as the point of measurement. In a typical car radio the i-f is 262 kHz. This means that the local oscillator should run at a frequency 262 kHz above the frequency to which the radio is tuned. When the radio is tuned to the high end of the dial (typically 1620 kHz), the local oscillator should have a frequency of 1620 kHz plus 262 kHz or a total of 1882 kHz. Ideally this is the frequency that would appear on the DFC. Unfortunately, the capacitance of the cable to the DFC input will detune the local oscillator. Instead of 1882 kHz it will read a bit lower. This is, however, really unimportant to our purpose. The amount of change that will completely kill the reception of the radio is much greater than this error. Refer back to Fig. 11-11. If the trimmer capacitor or the 300-pF capacitor in parallel with the trimmer become open, the DFC will display a frequency close to 2100 kHz when the radio is tuned to the high end of the band. If the .01-μF emitter bypass capacitor opens, the DFC will read close to 2500 kHz. The DFC lets you know not only the local oscillator frequency but also which component to suspect if that frequency should be incorrect.

Chapter 12

Car Radio Alignment

Of all the jobs performed by the automotive electronics technician, none is more technical or requires more skill than radio alignment. In the next few pages we will devote our efforts to demonstrating the basics of proper alignment.

A-M RADIOS

The simple a-m radio is, perhaps, the easiest to align. The test equipment is both simpler and less costly than that needed for either fm or stereo multiplex alignment. A service-grade rf signal generator covering the range of 200 to 1600 kHz is the instrument required to create the necessary controlled local signal. A good alternative is a crystal oscillator featuring switch-selectable outputs at 262.5 kHz, 455 kHz, and 500 kHz. If a large number of European radios are to be serviced also, the technician should have a unit with 460 kHz available. Specified frequencies are 262.5 kHz for the standard U.S. car radio i-f, 455 kHz for the i-f in all home radios and some older car radios, 460 kHz for the standard European i-f, and 500 kHz for a dial point marker. The harmonics of the 500-kHz crystal will identify the low end of the a-m band, the midpoint at 1000 kHz, and a high point of 1500 kHz. It is also possible to use a 1000-kHz crystal feeding a chain of IC frequency dividers to gain the required markers. A single J-K flip-flop will divide by two and produce 500 kHz. A decade divider IC or four J-K flip-flops connected as a module-10 divider will give you 100-kHz check points.

The second piece of equipment needed is some means of measuring relative output. This can be either an oscilloscope or ac vtvm across the speaker terminals. If this system is chosen, however, it is

necessary to use a modulated signal generator. Also, when using this system it might be wise to load the output of the radio with a power resistor, rather than a speaker. It can be rather nerve racking if several technicians are working close together. The silent approach to alignment will assist in keeping peace in the shop. A proper resistor for most car radios would have a value of 8 to 10 ohms at 10 watts.

Another useful signal level indicator is a dc vtvm connected across points affected by the automatic gain control (agc) circuit of the radio. In radios using an npn rf stage, connect the vtvm from either the agc control line to ground or the emitter of the rf amplifier transistor to ground. In radios using pnp transistors, connect the vtvm from the rf collector to ground. Or, connect the negative vtvm lead to the radio B+ line and the positive vtvm lead to the rf transistor emitter. The collector connection is both easier and more acceptable.

In any event, it is necessary to keep the rf output from the generator low enough to prevent the agc from upsetting your indications. Up to a certain point, the agc causes a linear decrease in the conduction of the rf amplifier transistor. Beyond that point, however, the radio will not reduce the gain in proportion to the signal level. This is called the *agc saturation point* or, more simply, the *agc knee.*

Most rf signal generators offer a 50-ohm output impedance. In most brands of signal generators, this figure is relatively resistive at low frequencies. Most car radios, however, use an antenna input impedance somewhat higher than 50 ohms. Because of this, it is necessary to simulate both the

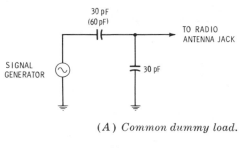

(A) Common dummy load.

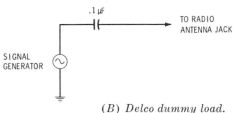

(B) Delco dummy load.

Fig. 12-1. Dummy (antenna) loads.

input impedance of the radio and the capacitive effects of the antenna feedline. Although the antenna cable has a lower capacitance than normally used in radio work, it still must be considered. This capacitance is shunted across the capacitor that tunes the input tank circuit in the radio. To compensate for the different capacitance values and to match the generator to the radio, you generally should use a dummy (antenna) load such as that illustrated in Fig. 12-1A. The value of the shunt capacitor is usually 30 pF. The series capacitor, however, tends to vary from brand to brand. In some it is specified as either 30 or 60 pF; others require more unusual values. The particular value required for any specific model car radio will be found in either the manufacturers service manuals or the Howard W. Sams AR-series PHOTOFACT books. Delco recommends using the dummy load shown in Fig. 12-1B. Although this will allow only

a rough adjustment of the antenna trimmer capacitor, it is best to use the manufacturer's specification on Delco radios. All of these dummy loads can be built into standard Motorola plugs universally used as the car radio antenna connector.

Fig. 12-2 shows the proper hookup of test equipment for aligning a typical a-m car radio. The signal generator will be connected to the antenna jack in most cases. In some instances, however, it is necessary to connect the generator output through a .1-μF capacitor to the base of the converter transistor for proper i-f alignment. A power line voltage meter is an optional but useful accessory. It is wise to insure that this voltage is set for the value actually found in the car. Standard voltages vary from car to car but will be indicated in the service literature.

From a procedural point of view, it is necessary to begin with the i-f amplifier. While remembering to keep the rf level just high enough to get a reasonable indication, peak the tuning cores of the i-f transformers. Start with the secondary tuning core on the output i-f transistor. Next, align the primary core of the same transformer. Proceed next to the secondary core of the input i-f transformer. Finish with the primary core of the input i-f transformer. After peaking all of the i-f transformers go back and repeat the process several times until no further increase in signal level can be produced. This is necessary because there is a certain amount of interaction between the various tuned circuits. If the radio is badly out of alignment, it will prove necessary to reduce the generator output several times during the course of alignment.

The front end of the radio is aligned by feeding the signal into the antenna circuit. The first step

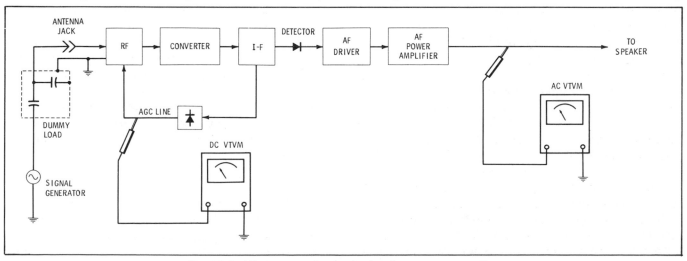

Fig. 12-2. Alignment equipment hookup for an a-m car radio.

is to set the oscillator tracking. Pick a generator frequency of known accuracy that corresponds to a frequency marking on the dial of the radio (1500 kHz is a good one on most radios). If the accuracy of your signal source is unknown, try using a broadcast station signal for this adjustment. The FCC requires a-m stations to maintain their frequency to within 20 Hz of the channel assignment. When both the radio and the generator are dialed in to the same frequency, adjust the oscillator trimmer capacitor for maximum signal as read by your level meter. This sets the oscillator frequency so that it tracks with the dial frequencies. If the tracking changes between the low end of the band and the high end, it will be necessary to adjust the LC ratio between the oscillator capacitance and inductor. The standard procedure is to adjust the trimmer for high-end tracking and the coil slug for low-end (600 kHz) tracking. The final step is to peak the rf amplifier collector and antenna tuning capacitors for maximum output. These steps must be repeated several times to insure accuracy.

The antenna peaking must also be repeated when the radio is remounted in the car and whenever changes are made to the antenna system of the car. One purpose for this trimmer is to compensate for variations from one antenna to another. If it is not performed in the car, the radio will remain tuned either to your bench antenna or your dummy load with the usual decrease in performance from the user's point of view. The trimmer adjustment is frequently omitted by the car dealer mechanics who install new radios. If a brand new radio is presented for repair and it appears to have either antenna or rf amplifier troubles, try peaking the trimmer before removing the radio from the car. This adjustment is made on a weak station above 1400 kHz. The trimmer capacitor adjustment will be found either on the chassis beside the antenna jack or behind both the front panel and control knobs.

FM RADIOS

Fm alignment can be performed in one of two ways. One uses a sweep generator and the other uses the unmodulated generator. Of the two methods, the sweep generator procedure is preferred if suitable test equipment is at hand. A cheap sweep generator, however, can negate your efforts enough to make the unswept method more successful.

The dummy antennas shown in Fig. 12-3 are usually recommended by the various radio manufacturers. The two-resistor dummy antenna in

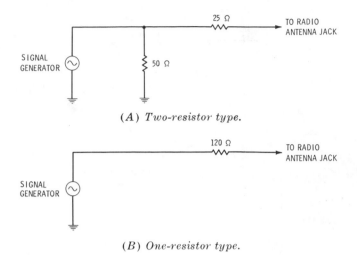

(A) *Two-resistor type.*

(B) *One-resistor type.*

Fig. 12-3. Dummy antennas for an fm car radio.

Fig. 12-3A offers a better match to the 50-ohm output that is common on rf signal generators. The capacitive dummy antenna used on a-m alignment will attenuate the signal too much and detune the fm radio input.

Also needed in fm alignment, especially if the sweep generator procedures are being used, are suitable oscilloscope and vtvm probes. One primary probe used in many applications, including alignment, is the low-capacitance probe. This style probe, illustrated in Fig. 12-4, consists of a 10-megohm resistor shunted by a 30-pF trimmer capacitor. The trimmer is adjusted for optimum performance by feeding a square wave through the probe to an oscilloscope. In most applications a 1000-hertz square wave is specified. The trimmer is adjusted until the squarest waveform is presented on the screen of the oscilloscope. The probe features a 10:1 attenuation ratio, which means the scope will display one-tenth the actual voltage applied to the probe. This is important to keep in mind when using such a probe. This probe can either be homemade, or it can be purchased for less than ten dollars in kit form.

Fig. 12-5 shows two demodulator probes used in fm alignment. The passive probe of Fig. 12-5A is the usual type employed. This probe also has an attenuation factor. The one redeeming quality of this style probe is that it is both effective and low

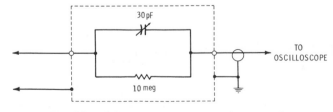

Fig. 12-4. Schematic of a low-capacitance probe.

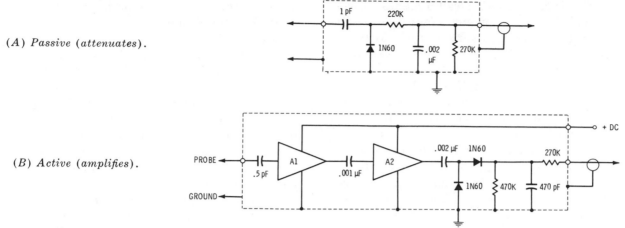

(A) Passive (attenuates).

(B) Active (amplifies).

Fig. 12-5. Two types of demodulator probes.

in cost. The more complex probe of Fig. 12-5B is becoming increasingly popular. It does away with the attenuation factor and, in fact, offers amplification. Specific circuits for this style of probe can be found in the service literature of appropriate radio manufacturers. The transistor amplifiers A1 and A2 are capacitively coupled. Simple stages using either bipolar or junction field-effect transistors (JFETs) can be employed providing they have a wide frequency response. These probes must respond to at least the fm i-f frequency of 10.7 MHz. It is desirable that the probe also provide at least some gain greater than unity up to the fm local oscillator maximum frequency of 120 MHz. This last, however, is a desirable option and is not mandatory in most instances, since the majority of all measurements will be made in the fm i-f amplifier stages.

Fig. 12-6 shows the basic equipment hookup for performing an fm alignment using an unmodulated signal source. The signal generator can be a simple service-grade instrument providing that it has reasonably decent short-term stability and has the capability of turning off the internal (usually a-m) modulation. One problem associated with using low-cost signal generators is the poor dial accuracy that occurs at both 10.7 MHz and vhf. Also, most of these instruments use harmonics to provide the frequencies above 20 or 30 MHz. This can be a problem if those harmonics are of insufficient strength. An alternative is to use a small transistorized crystal-controlled oscillator. The output buffer amplifier should be of sufficient power to give harmonics reasonable strength. Also, the output should be distorted to raise the harmonic content of the waveform. This approach is

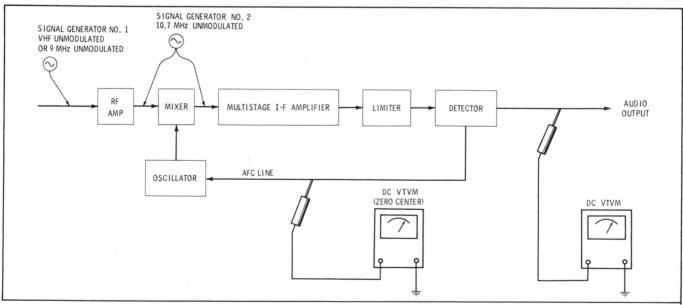

Fig. 12-6. Equipment hookup (nonsweep alignment) for an fm car radio.

preferred by at least one car radio manufacturer. The chapter on test equipment offers two designs that are suitable for this service. The oscillator will give both good stability and close control of frequency accuracy. The 10.7-MHz crystal is, of course, for fm i-f alignment. The 9-MHz crystal is used to provide fm band markers. Harmonics of 9 MHz will appear at 90, 99, and 108 MHz; this is perfect for most dial calibration purposes.

The rf signal should be injected into the system at the antenna jack via a suitable dummy antenna. The fm i-f signal can be injected in one of three places, depending upon convenience and the mechanical layout of the radio. One of the best places is the base of the mixer transistor. An alternate point is the base of the input i-f transistor or integrated circuit. Another alternative, if either of the two preferred points prove rather inaccessible, is illustrated in Fig. 12-7. That is, use a 2- or 3-inch piece of insulated hookup wire to *spray* the signal into the first fm i-f transformer. Two vtvm connections are needed. One is a zero center vtvm across the automatic frequency control (afc) line. The other is a normal vtvm across a point to ground where the dc level varies with signal strength. In some sets this will be in the detector, while in others it will be either the base or the emitter of the limiter transistor. Most bench vtvms can be made zero center simply by adjustment of the "zero" or "left marker" controls.

Fig. 12-8 shows a typical fm ratio detector circuit. Various alignment points are marked. The voltage across the a-m suppression capacitor (point C) will indicate the relative strength of the signal. The i-f transformers are peaked, using the voltage at this point as an indicator. The single most important adjustment is the secondary of the

detector transformer in both discriminator and ratio detector designs. This is generally done by monitoring the afc control line voltage. When the input signal is unmodulated, the voltage produced on this line will have a certain discrete level when no signal is present. This value in most sets is zero. When any frequency other than 10.7 MHz is present, or when the detector transformer secondary is misaligned, there will be either a positive or negative voltage generated. This generation depends on whether the error is above or below the design frequency. The secondary of the detector transformer is adjusted while monitoring the afc line with a zero center meter. At the same time, a 10.7-MHz continuous signal is applied to the input of the i-f amplifier strip. Adjust the core of the transformer secondary for zero voltage along this line.

The i-f transformers are aligned by adjusting their slugs while monitoring the signal level at an appropriate point. Peak the transformers for maximum signal level at the output. Again, the signal generator should be unmodulated. Use the 9-MHz crystal to align the fm local oscillator. Set the tuner to either the 90-, 99-, or 108-MHz dial calibration points. Monitor the afc control voltage with a zero center meter. Turn either the local oscillator coil adjustment or trimmer capacitor adjustment (depending upon the recommendation of the set maker) until the signal from the crystal oscillator or signal generator is centered in the passband of the radio. This will be indicated by the "zero" reading on the voltmeter. It may be necessary to begin the alignment procedure on a higher voltmeter scale and then repeat the process on lower scales until no further accuracy can be realized. As the adjustment is turned back and forth

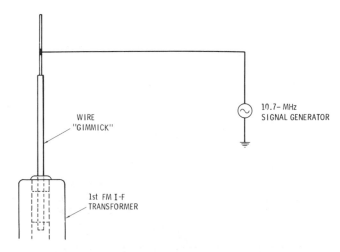

Fig. 12-7. "Gimmick" used to spray signal into fm i-f.

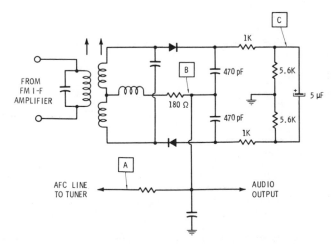

Fig. 12-8. Typical fm ratio detector circuit.

across the proper point, the zero center voltmeter will deflect first in one direction and then in the other. This indicates that the performance of the detector is normal.

The crystal oscillator output will probably be too high for accurate alignment of the rf amplifier trimmers. Most of the better quality vhf signal generators, however, have a variable attenuator capable of reducing the output sufficiently to perform these adjustments. In a pinch you can use a weak signal off the air for this step. Peak the trimmers for maximum signal output.

One good method for equipment hookup during sweep alignment of an fm car radio is shown in Fig. 12-9. Besides the sweep generator you will need a marker generator. This signal source will ideally produce both a 10.7 MHz and 100-kHz signals. The 10.7-MHz signal is needed to identify the center of the i-f passband. The 100-kHz markers help locate subsidiary points within that passband. The three signals, 10.7 MHz, 100 kHz, and the swept vhf fm signal, are combined in a piece of equipment called an adder. This device prevents interaction between the signals that could ruin the alignment. Some of the adders allow the two markers to appear on the scope trace horizontally so that they can be more easily identified. The current trend among test equipment makers is to incorporate all three items (sweep, marker, and adder) in one piece of equipment.

Fig. 12-10 shows the oscilloscope traces that will appear during fm alignment. Fig. 12-10A is the well-known discriminator S-curve that shows the varying response of the detector to frequencies within the receiver passband. The secondary (and to some extent the primary) of the fm detector transformer is adjusted for best symmetry of the S-curve. This curve, by the way, is taken across the discriminator output. The 10.7-MHz marker should be centered exactly on the zero line. The location of the other markers tends to vary somewhat from manufacturer to manufacturer. The

frequencies illustrated, however, are a reasonably common recommendation.

The passband curve shown in Fig. 12-10B is taken from the i-f amplifier. Ideally there will be no dip in the top portion of the curve. In reality however, there will be such a dip. This dip should be minimized during alignment so that it represents no more than ten percent of the total height of the curve as it appears on the scope screen. Another ideal rarely achieved is best symmetry and maximum height both occurring at the same adjustment points of the various i-f transformers. Where there has to be a trade-off between symmetry of the curve and overall height, make it a rule of thumb to choose symmetry over gain. This advice will hold true except in those areas that are a great distance from the nearest fm transmitter. Best symmetry of the curve will occur when the 6-dB frequencies are in the correct place. These frequencies may differ from one brand or model to another. Typical instructions for monaural are 150 to 200 kHz. A stereo fm receiver should have a wider bandpass to accommodate the higher frequency sideband products generated by the encoded stereo information. On these a passband with 6-dB points of 240 to 260 kHz are generally acceptable.

Stereo Section Alignment

Although it is frequently performed incorrectly, the alignment of the multiplex decoder is as simple as aligning an a-m radio. The principal tools are a stereo generator and an oscilloscope.

The chapter on test equipment details the type of test equipment needed. In brief, however, we will review the criteria. The stereo generator

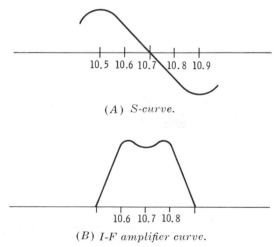

(A) S-curve.

(B) I-F amplifier curve.

Fig. 12-10. Two oscilloscope traces that appear during fm alignment.

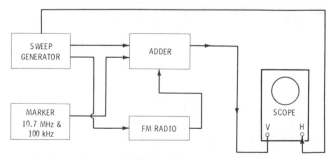

Fig. 12-9. Equipment hookup for sweep alignment of an fm radio.

should produce the needed 19 kHz, 38 kHz, and 67-kHz signals; a stereo composite and a vhf fm signal modulated by both the composite and the 19-kHz signals. The oscilloscope can be almost any audio type that will allow viewing signals up to 67 kHz. Just about every scope found in service shops will be more than sufficient for multiplex alignment.

The composite output of the multiplex generator can be injected directly into the stereo decoder input section. It would be better, however, to use it to modulate an fm generator (built into most multiplex generators) that feeds a signal to the antenna input. Otherwise the RC time constant of the decoder section input circuitry might change the composite signal enough to upset the alignment.

Adjust the SCA traps first. Modulate the generator with the 67-kHz audio signal. Place either the scope probe or the probe from an ac vtvm at point A in Fig. 12-11. Adjust the SCA trap so that a minimum (ideally none) signal appears at the test point. Next, switch the generator so that it produces a 19-kHz output. Place the scope probe at any of the points indicated in Fig. 12-11. Peak the 19-kHz and 38-kHz transformers for maximum signal. If the scope probe is placed at a point early in the chain, it must be moved further toward the decoder circuit with each subsequent adjustment. Repeat the process until an increase in signal levels cannot be obtained.

The secondary of the 38-kHz output transformer should be adjusted with a stereo generator produc-

ing either a *right only* or *left only* signal. The phase of the 38-kHz signal, as applied to the decoder matrix, has a profound effect on the degree of channel separation produced. Adjust the output transformer secondary so that a maximum signal is produced in the active channel and the signal in the *silent* channel in minimized. At this time, any separation controls being used should also be adjusted in the same manner.

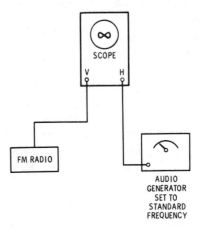

Fig. 12-12. Equipment hookup for aligning a 38-kHz phase-lock oscillator.

Certain older stereo designs used a phase-locked oscillator to generate the 38-kHz decoding signal. In these sets use oscilloscope Lissajous patterns to adjust the oscillator frequency (Fig. 12-12). Connect a sample of the 38-kHz signal to the vertical input of the oscilloscope. Connect the audio output of the stereo generator or the output of an accurate

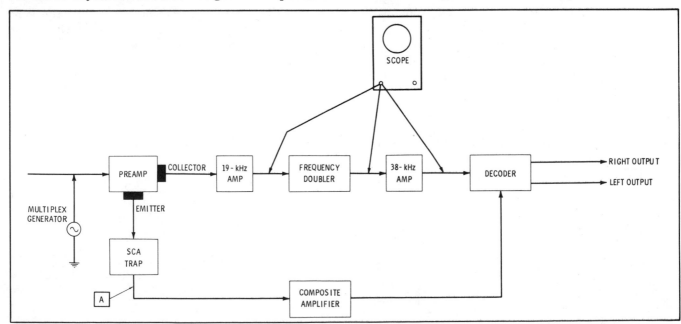

Fig. 12-11. Equipment hookup for stereo section alignment.

audio generator to the horizontal input of the scope. Set the external oscillator either to 38 kHz or to a frequency that is either a harmonic or sub-harmonic of 38 kHz. Suitable frequencies are 19 kHz, 38 kHz, or 76 kHz. Adjust the oscillator coil in the multiplex decoder until the Lissajous pattern on the screen of the oscilloscope locks in and remains stable. Tune the radio on and off several stereo stations (especially a weak station) to be sure that the oscillator will lock properly every time. If it does not, try adjusting the locked-oscillator coil until the real stable point is found.

Chapter 13

Tape-Player Troubles

The types of trouble found in both eight-track and cassette tape systems tend to be easily classified into only a few basic categories. Although there will surely be troubles which we cannot (for reasons of space) cover, the following are reasonably representative of the problems encountered in day-to-day servicing.

INCORRECT SPEED

One reason that many players are brought to the shop is that they run too slow. Most automotive tape players in both eight-track and cassette formats use a small, low power, dc motor connected to the flywheel via a rubber belt to supply the tape drive function. Almost any defect, electrical or mechanical, that affects this system will cause the player to lose speed.

There are several acceptable methods for determining whether or not a tape player is running at the correct speed. One method uses a mechanical strobe disc, printed with alternate bands of black and white. The number of bands is related to the frequency of the ac power mains in the area for which the strobe disc was designed. In the United States this means 60 Hz. When placed on the flywheel of a tape player and viewed under a fluorescent light source, the disc will produce a pattern of alternately colored bands. Most people claim that the bands are brownish-red and blue. Others, due to differences in their vision, will see other colors. The colored bands are caused by the fact that your vision is *strobed* by the fluorescent lights. This type of lamp turns on and off at a rate determined by the ac line frequency (60 Hz). Incandescent lamps also turn on and off sixty times per second.

They cannot be used for strobe work because the heated filament stays heated to a high brightness. Although the current source feeding the light turns on and off, the heated filament maintains an average brightness. Because of this only fluorescent lighting or small neon lamps can be used for tape player speed tests.

If the tape player is running at the proper speed, the color bands of the strobe will remain dead still. When the player speed is incorrect, however, the color bands will seem to rotate in one direction or the other. The direction of rotation determines whether the player is too fast or too slow, while the speed of rotation tells the magnitude of the speed error. It is worth noting that some manufacturers print a 60-Hz strobe pattern on either the flywheel or drive belts of their eight-track products. Cassette belts and flywheels are generally too small for such treatment.

Another popular method for checking tape player speed is to use one of the so-called *beeper* test tapes. Beeper tapes are usually recorded with a low-frequency tone (125 Hz is common) that is punctuated every 59 seconds with a 1000-Hz burst one second long. The effect is one beep per minute. A stop watch or a wristwatch with a sweep second hand is used to measure the time elapsing between successive bursts. The most accurate measurement is made using a stop watch. Time the beeps between successive trailing edges. If you are testing a player with what seems to be no, or a very small speed variation, let the test tape run for three complete minutes (a long time). If the stop watch shows, for example, a speed variation indicating that the machine gained (runs too fast) 2.4 seconds, you can assume a speed variation of .8 second per minute. This is well within tolerance for most machines. Most players are running normally if the beeps are plus or minus two seconds on a new test tape. This means that the beeps will appear every 58 to 62 seconds on a fresh tape assuming, of course, that the player is normal. As the tape gets a few months older, increase the tolerance to plus or minus three seconds or replace the tape. Most manufacturers build in a plus two-second speed error, so that as time passes and the player begins to slow down, it is still within their specified tolerance.

Fig. 13-1 illustrates another way to accurately measure the speed of a tape player. In this test are required a test tape recorded with a 60-Hz tone and an oscilloscope with the capability to be swept by and syncronized to the ac line. This feature is usually found on most low-cost oscilloscopes but

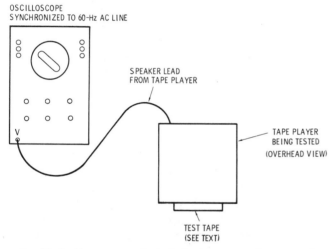

Fig. 13-1. Alternate method of checking tape-player speed.

may be missing on more expensive models. If you feed a 60-Hz signal from the ac line into the horizontal channel of the scope and the 60 Hz from the tape player into vertical amplifier input, the screen will display a Lissajous pattern. This pattern can be of several forms—a relatively straight line, an ellipse, or even a circle. The exact shape of the pattern is not too important except that it shows phase differences between the two signals. What is of importance is the stability of the pattern. When the player is running at precisely the correct speed, the tone fed to the oscilloscope will be exactly 60 Hz. This synchronizes with the line-derived 60 Hz being fed to the other scope channel to produce a steady Lissajous pattern. If the speed of the tape player is incorrect, the pattern will rotate. The speed and direction of rotation depend upon the direction and amount of speed error. It must

be assumed that there may be a small amount of error introduced by incorrect line frequency. These errors are typically small and of short duration. They will, however, cause a slow rotation of the Lissajous pattern, even when the player is running at the correct speed. Do not be too concerned if you average several seconds of beeper testing, only to find a very slow roll in the Lissajous pattern. This could easily be the result of line frequency problems.

Fig. 13-2 shows a newer method for determining tape-player speed. This is the test certain manufacturers are recommending for their newest and best equipment. In this method the indicating instrument is a digital frequency counter (DFC). A counter built from a low-priced kit is more than sufficient. To make this test, you need a test tape recorded with a tone between 300 and 1500 Hz. A good choice is 1000 Hz. With this frequency, a one-percent speed error exists for every 10 Hz of frequency error. As an example, let us assume that a

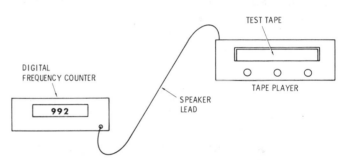

Fig. 13-2. Checking tape-player speed with a digital frequency counter.

given player produces a tone of 1014 Hz on the DFC during a speed test where a 1000-Hz reference tone was used. We can interpret this to mean that a 1.4 percent speed error exists. Since the DFC displayed frequently is higher than the reference, we know that it is 1.4 percent too fast. Test tapes for this purpose, especially in the cassette format, are available from many tape-player manufacturers. Contact the national service manager for those brands that you plan to service.

One required standard procedure on any tape equipment is regular cleaning. Tape oxide from one side of the tapes and powdered graphite from the other side will foul a machine in only a few dozen hours of playing time. This dirt and contamination must be cleaned out or the player may begin to run slow. The flywheel must be removed from its sleeve bearing and cleaned. It is also necessary to clean the internal surfaces of the sleeve bearing. Most tape players will use nylon or plastic bearings at one point or another. Because of this, avoid any cleaning solvent that harms plastic. A good solvent to use is isopropyl (rubbing) alcohol. Many of the commercial tape player solvents smell suspiciously similar to isopropyl alcohol. The difference in price, by the way, is upwards of several thousand percent. The best cleaning tools available are cotton swaps. You can obtain medical (sterile) swabs in any drug store. A savings in money and an increase in convenience is obtained by using nonmedical cotton swabs. These types are about four to six inches long and usually have wooden stems.

In lubricating a tape player, it is best to avoid going overboard. Excessive lubricant will not make things turn easier as might be supposed. In fact, the player will begin to slip and slow down if excessive lubricant is used. The best lubricant is a white grease such as *Lubriplate*. Only use white grease if the original manufacturer used a lubricant. Do not use oil on a tape player unless specifically directed by the tape player manufacturer. In any event, one drop of lightweight oil ("sewing machine" type) is all that will ever be used in any one player. Whatever lubricant is used, do not apply it to any point other than those indicated by the service manual. A good rule of thumb is never to lubricate any point where spillage or an excess can get to the tape. In most players this means using white grease (only) on the bottom capstan bearing and none on the top bearing. Even then, the lubricant must be used sparingly or not at all. If it is used to excess or in a sloppy manner it will ruin the first tape played in that machine. That first tape will most likely be your own expensive test tape.

Another common cause of slow speed is a defective motor. You can troubleshoot this problem best by inspection of the shaft speed with the drive belt disengaged. The motor should exhibit a fair amount of torque and should resume maximum speed rapidly after you manually cause it to stop rotating while power is still applied. A new replacement motor is usually the best service procedure. Fortunately, there are only a few basic tape-player motor assemblies within the two common formats. The number on the label applied to the motor core (inside the motor housing) gives the type number for the motor. This is a number used by the motor manufacturer. The motor manufacturer's number may or may not correspond to the numbering system used by the tape-player manufacturer. In the case where an off-brand tape player needs a motor, look for a motor from a ma-

jor manufacturer that has the same core number. It is most likely that you will find quite a few motors with the same number, unless that particular player uses an unusual motor. The author prefers to stock all of the different motors offered by the major tape-player manufacturers. This procedure results in a stock of fifteen basic motor types. Many technicians believe, however, that eight of the types will prove to be either dead stock or redundant stock.

Since most eight-track and some cassette tape players appear deceptively simple, many users are tempted to make minor adjustments themselves. This often results in an incorrect speed problem. Many tape players use a transistor to regulate the speed of the drive motor. These transistors are a frequent source of trouble and should be checked prior to making a motor replacement. It is mandatory that the circuit be analyzed to determine which kind of transistor defect will cause a specific symptom. If the transistor is a series regulator type, collector to emitter (C-E) leakage will cause the motor speed to increase. On the other hand, however, excessive C-E leakage will cause the motor speed to decrease in a shunt regulator circuit.

The drive belt is connected to the motor through a pulley of appropriate diameter. The pulley is attached to the motor shaft by set screws. If these set screws become loose, the pulley will slip and the motor will appear to be running slow.

The pulley is one part that should never be thrown away. Many tape players have reached a stage where they are fit only for salvage. In these cases retain the pulley and several other key parts before the remains are discarded. Keep parts such as the flywheel-capstan assembly and the flywheel sleeve bearings, unless the tape player is a common make for which parts are in abundant supply. One reason for retaining the pulley is that the one difference between an original motor and a replacement may be the speed of rotation. If you have a fair collection of different sizes of motor pulleys, you can make whatever changes are necessary until the correct combination of motor and pulley results in the correct speed.

One of the most common complaints in eight-track service is that the tape runs too fast. In most of these cases, the too-fast symptom is merely an indication that the machine has broken a tape. Examine the capstan. It may have several layers of tape wrapped neatly into a larger than normal diameter. This effectively increases the diameter of the capstan. It also reduces the ratio between the capstan and pinch-roller diameters causing an increase in speed. In most cases, clearing the extra tape from the machine will cure the problem. However, prior to inserting another tape into the machine, it would be wise to ascertain whether there are any defects that could break the tape. Monitor the tape carefully until you are certain that your own test tape is not in danger. The most common cause of tape breakage is, by the way, bad tapes, not bad tape players. It is excessive bearing friction that is usually at fault.

If the internal regulator switch (found in all tape player motors) fails, the motor will either stop or the speed will be close to double its normal value. One quick, although not always successful, troubleshooting procedure is to vigorously rap the tape player motor housing with the handle of a screwdriver or similar instrument. If the speed returns to normal then replace the motor. It may prove tempting to leave the old motor in the machine if the speed remains normal for a few minutes. However, this "repair" is only temporary. The motor will fail again shortly.

NOISE

One common and often unsolvable problem is noise pickup from the tape-player motor. The noise, a hash type of sound, will get into the audio stages and interfere with the program material. If the noise appears after a motor replacement, disassemble the motor housing to determine whether or not the metal noise shield is in place. If it is missing or is installed incorrectly, the motor will radiate noise that can be picked up as induced currents by the highly sensitive audio input circuits. A broken ground connection on the printed-circuit board can cause a ground loop that can introduce motor noise into the system. Such open circuits must be located and eliminated. Another very common cause of motor noise pick-up is input preamplifier lead dress. The most important lead to watch in this connection is the shielded head harness connecting the playback head to the preamplifier circuit. If this harness is dressed close to the motor or motor power wires, it may easily pick up stray noise fields. Some imported tape players were well-known for this type of problem. It would take about six months for the motor to deteriorate to a point where the problem was noticeable. The problem is generally traced to increased sparking across motor brushes shortened by age. Redressing the preamplifier input wires or replacing the motor would cure the problem.

CROSS TALK

Another common tape-player complaint is actually two-fold. The first part of the complaint concerns cross talk. It can be caused either by improper head height alignment or by defective tapes. (Print-through sounds exactly like cross talk most of the time.) The other part of this two-fold problem is loss of high-frequency response due to misalignment of tape head azimuth. Fig. 13-3 reiterates the alignment steps necessary to resolve these problems. In both cases it is necessary to use an appropriate test tape to make the adjustment.

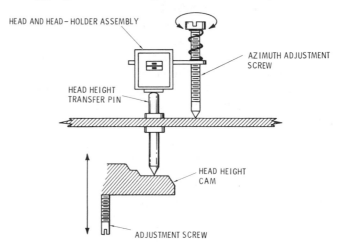

Fig. 13-3. Tape-player head-alignment adjustments.

A good cross-talk test tape will have a low-frequency tone recorded on either side of a blank track. This is the so-called *null* cross-talk test. The azimuth test tape, for high-frequency response tests, will be recorded with a tone in the 6- to 8-kHz range. The tone in the cross-talk test is nulled to zero while the tone in the azimuth procedure is peaked for maximum. In either case do both alignments and do them twice to insure against interaction. There are still some older style test tapes available in which you peak a tone for cross-talk adjustments. With null method you can use your ears as the indicator. In the peak method, however, you should use either an oscilloscope or an ac vtvm for an indicator.

LOSS OF FREQUENCY RESPONSE

Improper playback head care is another common cause of poor high-frequency response. Oxide contamination on the head is responsible for many complaints of high-frequency loss. Cleaning the head with an approved chemical cleaner is the best cure. A better job will be afforded by manually cleaning the head with a solvent and a cotton swab rather than by using one of the head cleaner tapes. Such cleaning tapes are useful for maintaining a low residue of oxide, but they are far too inefficient for professional use or after the oxide has already built up beyond the point where it affects performance.

Is is also necessary to periodically demagnetize the head and all other metal parts that run in direct contact with the tape surface. A good demagnetizer placed against the metal parts for a short period of time as specified by the manufacturer will do the trick. The results of demagnetization will be better if the wet technique is used. Place the tip of the demagnetizer against one side of a small piece of cloth that has been soaked in head cleaning solvent. Move the cloth and demagnetizer around the surface of the head in a circular motion for a few moments. This will loosen and remove bits of embedded iron oxide missed by a normal head cleaning.

EIGHT-TRACK TROUBLES

Some players use an electromagnet to hold the tape cartridge pinch arm in place. Many machines using either the electromagnet or a purely mechanical eject system will not play specific brands of tape cartridge. Most eight-track players are designed to play only the original Lear-Jet style cartridges. If the machine has an adjustment that allows variation in the pinch-arm mechanism, it may be possible to find a point where all, or at least most, of the cartridges will play. In the case of electromagnetic types it is the front-to-back position of the solenoid that counts. When this position is varied, it is usually necessary to readjust the angular position so that it continues to sit flush with the operating level.

The track change system in eight-track tape players is subject to enough use and abuse to provide a high failure rate. In most designs, the track change (TC) circuit consists of a manual TC switch, an automatic TC switch (sense contacts), a solenoid magnet, and a spike suppression diode. Most trouble will be either in the manual or automatic TC switch. In the case of the manual switch, replacement is the usual repair procedure. The auto TC switch, however, consists of a pair of metal contacts that ride in contact with the tape. The aluminum foil used to splice together the ends of the endless loop tape will short these contacts together, thereby completing a circuit to ground. If tape oxide is allowed to build up on the TC

switch, it may cause either an open (if the oxide is on the surface) or a short (if it gets between the contacts). Fig. 13-4 illustrates the latter. The shorted condition will cause the solenoid to stay energized. This can and often does cause the solenoid to burn out.

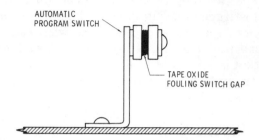

Fig. 13-4. Oxide fouling of the automatic track change switch.

The cam which is used to set the head height can also be defective once it gets worn. If the wear is bad enough, the head will be lowered sufficiently enough to present permanent cross talk. If the cross talk is adjusted out, you may lose one track of either program. (Track one or four will be lost, depending upon the design of the machine.) A similar problem can occur if the tension spring that drives the head carriage loses some of its power. The head will tend to rest at a point close to its normal position but far enough out to cause cross talk.

CASSETTE TROUBLES

Most troubles that beset cassette players are troubles that are common to all three tape formats. There are, however, a few that are unique to cassette systems. One of these is tape spill. There are two forces that drag the tape inside the cassette from the supply reel to the take-up reel. One of these is the rotation of the take-up reel and spindle while the other is the rotation of the capstan pinch-roller assembly. If the take-up reel loses some of its tension, then the tape will tend to back up between the reel and the capstan. When the backup reaches a point of excessive slack, the tape will spill out of the cassette. Then, it usually snags the pinch-roller assembly and will break. This symptom can be caused either by a warped capstan or by insufficient tension in the take-up reel assembly. In most cases, the reel will have stopped completely, while in others it simply will have begun to slip. Measure the tension with a gram scale and a cassette adapter. Most players will have between 40 and 60 grams of take-up tension. Since excessive tension can also cause tape breakage, readings in excess of 100 grams should be investigated closely.

The other unique cassette problem is premature ejection on Staar system machines. Staar patent machines are those that are slot loaded. Most of these use an end-of-play sensor on the electrical eject system. A pair of sense brushes or a rotating sense magnet will supply pulses to a sense amplifier whenever the supply reel is turning. If a wire is broken or if the sense brushes become worn or corroded, the amplifier will no longer receive the pulses. In a normally functioning player most sense amplifiers eject the cassette in eight or ten seconds after the pulses cease. If the mechanism is defective, the cassette will be ejected eight to ten seconds after it is inserted. Curing this problem can be as simple as cleaning or readjusting the sense brushes. In other cases it might be necessary to replace the brushes and even the wheel attached to the supply reel.

Chapter 14

Noise Suppression

Automotive electronic equipment must operate in an environment of high electrical and electromagnetic noise levels. Proper design of the equipment can make it less susceptible to noise interference. In the final analysis, however, it is the service technician who must bear the responsibility for noise suppression. His job begins when the radio and the car have been joined together to work as a system.

IDENTIFYING THE SOURCE

Normally, the first step in any noise suppression procedure is to identify the source of the noise. Once this is known, appropriate corrective measures can then be taken. Table 14-1 lists information about the major and most common forms of noise encountered in automotive systems.

A static or popping sound can be produced by the spark plugs and ignition system. Electrical sparks are such efficient sources of rf energy that early radiocommunications pioneers used a *spark gap* as a type of radiotelegraph transmitter. It is no wonder, then, that the spark gaps in your ignition system can be the source of interference to radio reception. Ignition noise has a repetition rate that varies with the speed of the engine. The exact repetition rate is a function of the number of cylinders in the engine and the number of revolutions per minute the engine is turning at the time.

The older style automotive battery charging systems used a dc generator that was belt-driven from the engine. These generators would produce a whine in the radio output. This would be similar to the now-familiar alternator whine but was a far less pure tone. In both cases, however, the whine

is high-pitched and will tend to vary with engine speed variations. The change is generally much more pronounced than are changes in the repetition rate of ignition system static.

Another source of a whining type of interference are any dc motors used to drive such devices as the heater blower, power seats, and power windows. The motors are generally high-speed affairs with reduction gearing suitable for the intended use. Although a sound is difficult to describe, there is sufficient difference between these types of whines to keep you from mistaking one for the other. One of the other characteristics of whine produced by dc motors is that it will vary only slightly or not at all with changes in engine speed.

The old-style voltage regulator, an electromechanical affair, produced a peculiar type of interference often described as resembling the sound of frying eggs. This interference is difficult to troubleshoot because it is intermittent. It is often necessary to depend upon the customer's description rather than your own observation. One test to isolate a noise such as regulator hash is to create a heavy current drain on the battery. This can be accomplished most quickly by turning on the headlights and switching them to the high-beam position. This heavy drain will close the offending regulator contacts, causing the noise to cease. If this drain causes the noise either to disappear or change radically, then the regulator is at fault.

Another problem occurring with some degree of regularity is a random popping that seems to both intensify and increase in repetition rate when the car is subjected to vibration. A possible source for this type of interference is the gasoline sensor mechanism that drives the gas gauge. The test for

Table 14-1. Types of Radio Interference

Noise Produced	Cause	Cure	Remarks
Static	Ignition system	See text.	Repetition rate varies with engine speed.
Whine	Generator	A .5-μF capacitor from armature to ground.	Pitch varies with engine speed.
Whistle	Alternator	See text.	Pitch varies with engine speed.
Hash (frying eggs)	Electromechanical voltage regulator	A .5-μF capacitor from battery terminal to ground (see text).	Noise often disappears when headlights are turned on.
Whirring noise	Electric motors (blower, etc.)	A .5-μF capacitor from power lead to ground.	
Irregular popping	Gasoline gauge	A .5-μF capacitor from sensor wire to ground See manufacturer's service manual.	Rate changes when car is rocked.

this type of noise is to gently rock the car back and forth from side to side a few inches. This should be done with the engine off but the ignition key in the "on" position. If the noise speeds up as the car is rocked, then assume that the noise source is the gas gauge circuit. This noise is often appropriately described as a "sloshing sound" by customers.

There are numerous other sources of noise interference to car radio reception. Some of them are impossible to actually cure. If the customer complains that passing cars interfere with his reception the only cure is to attempt to get him to increase his signal-to-noise ratio by tuning to a stronger station.

Loose body parts or a loose antenna can also generate a type of noise. In most cases tightening the loose part is the proper cure. Some modern cars, however, use a putty-like antirattle compound between major body parts and between the dashboard and the firewall. These can allow the associated body parts to float above actual dc ground as far as the rf noise is concerned. A resistance check with an ohmmeter will detect close to zero ohms resistance between the radiating member and the chassis. To rf, however, that fraction of an ohm which your meter has difficulty resolving may

prove significant. The only cure for this noise source is to bypass the putty with half-inch wide bonding braid. This braid jumper must be kept as short as possible, especially if high-frequency communications or fm broadcast receivers are being affected.

ELIMINATING THE NOISE

Fig. 14-1 shows the power-supply section of a typical modern car radio. Three of the parts used in this supply circuit are for the express purpose of eliminating noise pulses that enter via the power line (the 200-pF spark plate, the 1-henry choke coil, and the 1000-μF capacitor). If the choke shorts out or if the 1000-μF capacitor opens, the radio will exhibit noise. One method for checking the radio in the car is to bridge a 1000-μF 25-V dc capacitor between the power line and ground. If this either attenuates or eliminates the noise altogether, remove the radio for bench service. In most cases a subjective determination can be made by noting the character of the interference. If there are several types of interference present, then the power-supply suppression circuitry is the suspect. If, on the other hand, there is only one type of noise present, look to the appropriate source for the trouble.

As a car gets older, some of the devices that had been previously quiet will begin to produce more noise than the power-supply filters can remove effectively. In these cases it may be desirable to increase the filtering. Two networks that have proved effective in the past are shown in Fig. 14-2. In Fig. 14-2A we have a simple L-section filter. The

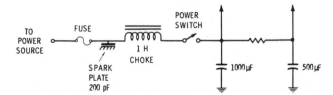

Fig. 14-1. Typical power-supply input circuit of a modern car radio.

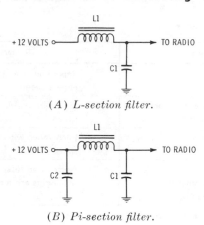

(A) *L-section filter.*

(B) *Pi-section filter.*

Fig. 14-2. Typical filter networks.

capacitor, C1, can be either a .5-μF, 200-V dc auto suppression type or a 1000-μF, 25-V dc electrolytic. The higher value capacitor is used only in the most severe cases and when breaker-point flutter is a problem. Inductor L1 has a value close to 1 henry. This coil is a standard input choke for a car radio and may be obtained from replacement stock. In cases of only ignition noise it is sometimes permissible to use a homemade choke of considerably less inductance. Approximately 20 turns of No. 22 hookup wire wrapped around a 1.5 inch length of 3/8-inch diameter ferrite antenna should do the trick. In the more severe cases, use the 1 henry choke. The filter of Fig. 14-2B is called a pi section after its schematic resemblance to the Greek letter π. This filter is only used in the most severe cases. The parts specifications are the same as for the L section.

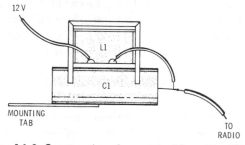

Fig. 14-3. Construction of a practical L-section filter.

Fig. 14-3 shows the construction of a practical L-section filter. In this version, a choke is soldered to a noise suppression capacitor. Either the side tab or end tab type of capacitor may be used in this application. It is, however, important that the capacitor be of the type specified for car radio noise elimination.

Fig. 14-4 shows several types of noise suppression capacitors. Fig. 14-4A illustrates the end mount style. In this capacitor type, the value will

be between .1 and .5-μF at 200 V dc. Fig. 14-4B shows a capacitor that is electrically identical to that of 14-4A. The location of the mounting tab is the only difference. The amount of space is the factor which determines where the tab is placed. The case of both types is made from tinned steel which takes solder rather easily. Most noise elimination capacitors will have the usual spade lug attached to the lead wire. You will find other connectors, however, on capacitors supplied by certain manufacturers for specific automobiles. Certain German cars, for example, use capacitors with a double push connector that has both male and female spade lugs. This is useful for quick connection to Bosch ignition coils.

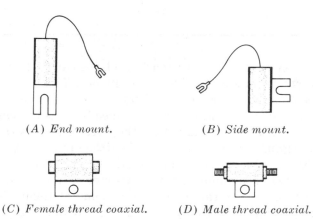

(A) *End mount.*   (B) *Side mount.*

(C) *Female thread coaxial.*   (D) *Male thread coaxial.*

Fig. 14-4. Noise suppression capacitors.

Fig. 14-4C shows a coaxial type capacitor with female threaded bushings. The male threaded bushing type is shown in Fig. 14-4D. Coaxial bypass capacitors are considered superior to the other types at frequencies above 2 MHz and where noise interference is particularly severe.

Fig. 14-5 shows the schematic of a typical automobile ignition system. This basic system has been in use for the greater part of automotive history with only minor modification. Transformer T1 has a high turns ratio that converts the 12-volt dc to a high voltage in excess of 15,000 volts. The system operates by a set of breaker points that are opened and closed by a cam driven from inside the engine. When the switch points close, dc will flow through the windings of the primary (left) side of T1, magnetically energizing the entire coil. When the cam opens the points a fraction of a second later, the magnetic field built up around the coil begins to collapse. This induces a current into the secondary winding. The high turns ratio between the primary and secondary windings causes this current to create the high voltage needed to fire the spark plugs. Capacitor C1 is used to prolong breaker point life by reducing some of the arcing that will occur and to aid the collapse of the magnetic field by discharging through T1.

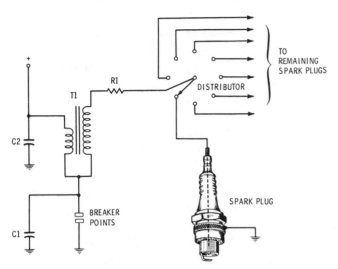

Fig. 14-5. Schematic of a typical automobile ignition system.

The distributor is actually a rotary switch that is turned by the engine. It distributes the high voltage to each spark plug in the proper sequence and at the proper time. A degree of noise suppression is offered by C2 and R1. Capacitor C2 is one of the standard automotive noise suppressors described previously. Resistor R1 can be a separate resistor, or it can be plugged on to either the spark plugs or the high tension-wires. In most modern cars, the resistor is in the form of resistive high-tension leads to each spark plug. This type of spark plug wire uses a carbon impregnated nylon filament in place of the normal copper (low resistance) wire. This type of wire can have a total resistance between 10,000 ohms and 100,000 ohms. It will be identified on the outer insulation by wording

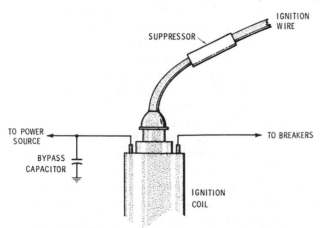

Fig. 14-6. Placement of noise suppressor (resistor).

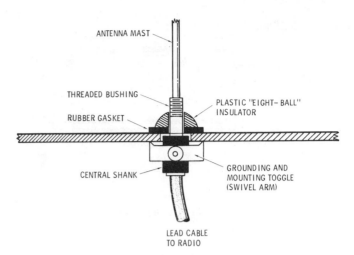

Fig. 14-7. Cross section of car radio antenna showing grounding system.

such as "radio," "radio-tv suppression," or "resistance wire." This wire deteriorates after awhile and may, itself, become a source of noise. Regular replacement at approximately two-year intervals is usually recommended both from the radio interference point of view and engine efficiency point of view.

Fig. 14-6 shows how an external resistor can be added to the ignition system to eliminate noise. The resistors used are specifically designed for this job. Most of them consist of a black plastic cylinder filled with carbon. The usual place for the resistor is in the high-tension lead between the ignition coil and the distributor. It should be physically as close to the coil as possible. There are types available (at a slightly higher cost) that fit right inside the high tension *tower* connector of the ignition coil.

The car radio antenna system uses a type of coaxial cable between the mast mounted to the fender of the car and the radio input connector. This shield must be well grounded at both ends if noise is to be avoided. A common mistake made while installing new antennas is the failure to remove paint and undercoating from the underside of the fender around the antenna mounting hole. In these cases, the mounting toggle (Fig. 14-7) cannot make a good ground, and noise interference will be the likely result. It is also possible to have a broken ground either inside the antenna base assembly or the cable and connectors. If this occurs, replacement of the offending piece, or in some instances the whole assembly, is in order.

The high-pitched variable whine produced by the generator can usually be suppressed by the use of a simple bypass capacitor. This is illustrated in

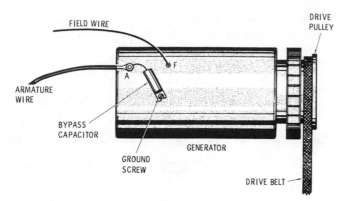

Fig. 14-8. Installing a bypass capacitor on a generator.

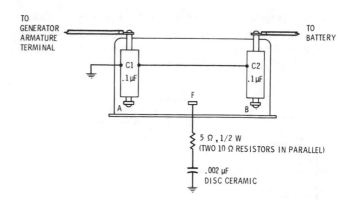

Fig. 14-10. Suppression techniques for excessive regulator hash.

Fig. 14-8. Use a .5-μF capacitor connected between the armature terminal and ground. In really severe cases it may be necessary to use a coaxial type rather than the tab-mounted. It is mandatory that the capacitor be connected to the armature wire on the generator rather than to the field wire. The wire from the armature can be easily identified by its size; it will be at least twice the size of the field wire.

In the case of an alternator it is necessary to refer to the manufacturer's service literature before attaching any bypass capacitors. This is due to the fact that the precise value of the bypass capacitor can be critical. It is possible to choose a value accidentally that will tune the alternator coil to a frequency in resonance with one of the frequencies produced by the alternator at a specific engine speed. Since extremely high currents can flow inside a parallel-resonant tank circuit, this can destroy either the alternator winding or the associated rectifier diodes. The manufacturer's service updates or manuals will give instructions applicable to his products. It is worth noting that alternator noise which suddenly appears in a previously quiet installation may mean either trouble with the alternator or in the radio input circuit.

Fig. 14-9 illustrates how to suppress electric motor noise by installing a .5-μF capacitor on the power line. The real job is to get to the power lead

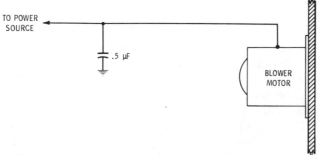

Fig. 14-9. Capacitor placement to suppress dc motor noise.

at a point close enough to the motor to do some good. For one reason or another most dc motors tend to be placed in the most inconvenient locations. The heater and air conditioner blower motor can sometimes be approached from the engine side of the firewall. In most cars, and on most motors, the task of approaching the motor is somewhat complicated.

Normally the voltage regulator noise is easy to suppress. First, try connecting a .5-μF bypass capacitor between the battery terminal of the regulator and ground. If this is unsuccessful, it may be necessary to use the techniques illustrated in Fig. 14-10. The field terminal is to be treated only in the manner shown unless the manufacturer makes specific recommendations. Make a series RC network consisting of two 10-ohm, half-watt resistors paralleled to make a 5-ohm combination in series with a .002-μF disc ceramic capacitor. It might be worth noting that some car manufacturers supply this circuit already made up and encapsulated in either bakelite or epoxy/fiberglass. If this circuit is used, the mounting tab is also the ground connection. The battery and generator (alternator) terminals are bypassed with coaxial type .5-μF capacitors. The 10-32 thread used in the bushings of most female coaxial capacitors is the same size used on most voltage regulator terminals. A 10-32 stud made from a machine screw can be used to connect the capacitor bushing and the regulator terminal. The wire that had previously been connected to the regulator terminal must now be rerouted to the other end of the bypass capacitor. Connect the bodies of the two capacitors together and to ground with a piece of half-inch bonding braid. According to the usual practice, make the braid as short as possible without straining the regulator terminals or the capacitor.

Most other devices on the car that can create

radio noise may be treated with a .5-μF bypass capacitor, or, if they are really severe or stubborn, a coaxial type can be used. Always keep in mind that the appearance of radio interference from a particular source may mean that a defect is developing which may require further investigation by a mechanic.

Remember that the first step in any noise suppression procedure is to identify the source. After the source has been identified, one may proceed with the job of eliminating the noise. Use Table 14-1 as much as possible to speed up your servicing. Keep to a good established procedure and even the most difficult problems can be solved.

Chapter 15

Reception Problems

An understanding of certain reception problems that are unique to automobile radio installations is needed by the servicing technician. This is one area where an understanding of the problem is of primary importance.

A-M RECEPTION

During the daylight hours the a-m band is normally restricted by the physics of radio propagation to local broadcasting. However, the useful range of a-m is different on the opposite ends of the band. Broadcasters really envy stations which have frequency assignments on the low end of the dial, because it means that the signal should carry farther for a given power authorization. It is not unusual to find 1-kilowatt low-end stations propagating farther than 5-kilowatt high-end stations. A range of 50 to 100 miles must be considered normal maximums for daytime in the a-m band. Of course, there will be a considerable number of stations which cannot even approach that figure.

Although range is short during the daylight hours, a curious thing begins to happen in the evenings. As the sun sets, the ionosphere begins to readjust. Since much of the noise on the a-m band is solar in origin, the noise level will tend to go down. During the evening and throughout the night until sunrise, reception distances will increase out to a thousand miles or more. East coast listeners will often hear stations located in the central or midwestern region of the country as well as foreign stations from Mexico, the Carribean, Central America and Canada. Long-distance reception does not affect most table-model home radio receivers because most of these units lack the required sensi-

tivity. Car radios, on the other hand, are better built and will usually have an rf amplifier, a feature missing on most home radios. In a car radio, that extra sensitivity, although a real blessing in isolated areas, can prove to be a problem at night. During the evening, the radio will be tuned to several stations at once on the same or adjacent channels. This is not a problem during the day because the radio will not pick up distant signals. Local channel assignments are separated enough so that interference will be minimal. At night, however, these adjacent channel signals will arrive and cause interference with each other. If the radio is tuned to 780 kHz at night, for example, it will pick up that signal plus a 770-kHz and a 790-kHz signal. These latter two will beat against the 780-kHz signal to produce 10-kHz heterodyne frequencies. Although the audio and i-f selectivity help reduce heterodyne interference, they do not completely eliminate the problem.

This problem does not normally occur during daylight hours because the adjacent channel stations simply are not being received. This does not rule out, however, the possibility of freak occurrences during which daytime interference does occur. On certain days, atmospheric conditions will be such that some signals can be quite loud and will be able to interfere with local reception. In these cases, the interference will be far worse than the nighttime variety because of the larger number of stations on the air.

The length of the antenna of an a-m car radio is only a few inches—far shorter than the length of a tuned antenna (200 to 600 feet) for the same frequency range. The antenna on a car radio is tuned by a small trimmer capacitor inside the radio. On some models this adjustment will be accessible by removing the tuning knob and the dummy knob. On others, it will be found close to the antenna jack on the radio chassis. The antenna trimmer adjustment is made with the mast fully extended and with the radio tuned to a weak signal that is near 1400 kHz. However, if a weak signal is not available, do not be tempted to use a strong signal. Because of the agc circuit, this will cause the peak point in the adjustment to be overly broad and therefore obscured. In preference to a strong station, use the interstation noise between 1400 and 1600 kHz as your test signal. If this adjustment is not made (and it is frequently overlooked by installers and other mechanics not familiar with radio problems), the radio will lack sensitivity. When this control is not adjusted properly, the passband of the radio may be increased. Such a misadjustment may also create high-frequency heterodynes by admitting adjacent signals that may otherwise be eliminated by the rf amplifier.

FM RECEPTION

Reception of fm is a little unusual. This must really be understood by the service technician so that he will be in a position to clear up some of the popular misconceptions held by the typical customer. Some of these ideas are: (1) fm is noise-free, (2) fm will not fade in tunnels, and (3) fm always provides better performance than a-m. Let us examine these ideas and try to pick out what is truth and what is hopeful dreaming.

The idea that noise does not affect fm is not entirely true. The statement must be qualified before it can be allowed to stand unchallenged. As with most of the misconceptions with which we will deal, there is a grain of truth that can be amplified to an untrue concept. If the signal present at the antenna terminals of the receiver is above a certain minimum level, the limiter circuits will clip off any amplitude variations present on the carrier. Since most forms of noise will tend to amplitude modulate the host carrier, it will be clipped off in the limiters. The limited fm signal, in this case, will be much quieter than any a-m signal. However, the if signal is too weak to drive the limiters effectively, no clipping will take place and the noise will ride on through. If the fm signal uses either the ratio or quadrature detectors, the noise susceptance will be minimal. Also to be considered is the fact that the encoded stereo signal (L − R) is amplitude modulated into a 38-kHz subcarrier. The subcarrier is suppressed, but the resultant double sideband (dsb) composite is frequency modulated on the transmitter carrier. The dsb composite can be susceptible to noise. The qualification on the susceptibility of the fm receiver to noise is that the set must be tuned to a station strong enough to drive the limiters into clipping. If the signal is weaker than this critical threshold, the set may be as noisy or even more noisy than an a-m radio.

As mentioned before, another misconception is that fm will not fade in tunnels. The short wavelengths associated with the fm band do reflect off hard surfaces and tend to bounce around downtown areas. This can be both a benefit and a disadvantage. If the bending and reflection is sufficient, the signals will penetrate underpasses and tunnels. Long tunnels, however, may allow fading. The big difference between a-m and fm in such cases is that the fm radio will continue playing far deeper into the tunnel.

There are other types of fading which will affect fm but not a-m. This is a contradiction to the generally held belief. One such type of fading is called *picket fencing*. This trouble is only present while the vehicle is in motion. The symptoms are a "pfft-pfft-pfft" noise as you drive along. If the radio is a stereo set, the lamp may also flicker at the same rate as the noise occurs. The problem here is cancellation zones. The easy tendency to bounce off buildings and other structures that allows fm to propagate in tunnels is, in part, responsible for this phenomenon. With so many signals arriving at the antenna due to multiple reflections, we have many urban and suburban areas that seem to be one continuous cancellation zone after another. If you drive through a series of cancellation zones in rapid succession, your radio will be alternately fed a very weak then a very strong signal. It is this that causes the *picket fencing* effect. Cancellation zones occur every few feet in areas where the problem is severe. It must be pointed out that similar symptoms can be caused by certain agc and local oscillator-to-mixer coupling problems.

The third and final major type of fading is caused by fm shadow zones. If a large structure, such as a multistory building, is positioned between the broadcast station and the fm receiver, there may be difficulty in reception. The only cure is to move out of the *shadow zone* (cancellation zone) into an area of higher signal strength. The physical size of the shadow zone is dependent upon many factors: (1) the size of the offending structure and its distance from the transmitter, (2) the height of the transmitter and receiver antennas with respect to the building size, and (3) the sensitivity of the radio and its distance from the building. All of these variables can contribute to the determination of cancellation zone size. The zone can vary from a few square feet to several miles.

Occasionally a cancellation or shadow zone will be found out in the middle of the countryside many miles from the nearest obstruction. The cause of this is usually a multipath condition where a direct and a reflected signal or two reflected signals converge on a particular point miles from the normal area where this might be expected. This condition will probably exist for only a short distance. There are places, though, where a dead zone has extended for several hundred yards.

Another misconception concerning fm automotive reception is the customer's idea of proper reception distances. Frequency modulation is said to have a line-of-sight service zone. This means line-of-sight between antennas rather than optical line of sight. However, this is an unfortunate misnomer. Just as an aviator can increase the distance coverage of his radio transceiver by climbing to a higher altitude, the fm system can get increased range by raising the antenna heights. This could mean higher antennas on both ends. Many texts give the term "horizon" as the limit for vhf reception. In actuality, the vhf signal will be usable out to a distance of about fifteen percent beyond the geographic horizon. After this point, the signal strength will drop off rapidly to a point where it is too weak to offer any reception.

Monaural broadcasts are easier to receive at great distances than are stereo broadcasts. One reason for this is that the stereo signal will modulate the fm transmitter by no more than ten percent. This will, of course, cause the encoded stereo signal to be much weaker than the mono signal when measured at the output of the detector. Because of this, reputable stereo car radio manufacturers will only claim to offer decent stereo reception out to a distance of 15 or 20 miles. The same station will produce decent monaural reception out to 25 or 30 miles. This is one argument in favor of a *stereo defeat* or *mono-stereo* switch on a car radio.

It is hard to convince a customer that his car radio will not perform up to his hi-fi at home. His elaborate fm stereo receiver will, of course, be connected to an expensive and very high-gain antenna system. It is natural to assume that such a step up will perform much better than even the finest car radio system. The customer, however, may not see this point. Within his limited experience, all he knows is that a certain distant station is audible at home but not in the car. Your treatment of this type of customer's problem will, it is hoped, be diplomatic.

For every case of normal fm reception distances we are likely to find another case of abnormal coverage. A station with super high power, a very tall antenna, or a very high-gain antenna will, of course, be able to cover a greater distance than a smaller station. There may be a question presented about why a certain station in a distant city is audible when others in the same city are either very weak or are totally inaudible. It would be wise for you to know the answers.

Also, there are several types of atmospheric activity that can cause vhf radio waves to propagate over abnormally long distances. One of these is the northern lights. These lights are actually highly ionized patches of sky seen usually in the northern latitudes. The ionization that results in a wildly dancing light display also forms a radio mirror that reflects back to earth signals that would have otherwise escaped into space. Meteor showers also cause intermittent long-distance vhf reception. One of the best is the Perseid shower that occurs every August. When the meteors hit the atmosphere, they leave an ionized trial that acts like a mirror much the same way as do the northern lights. One last type of intermittent vhf propogation is called the *sporadic E layer*. This occurs when the hot summer sun ionizes a low layer of the ionosphere called the *E layer*. The most frequent occurrence is during the months of June and July. During these months sporadic but rather surprising reception conditions occur. It is not too unusual for television and fm signal to propagate over a thousand miles. It may last only a few moments during any one episode but it will definitely be there.

Unusual fm antennas continue to be sold in relatively large numbers. In most cases an improvement in performance is promised but rarely delivered. The two most successful types of fm car radio antennas are the quarter-wavelength monopole whip and the half-wavelength dipole windshield antenna. The whip is a 32-inch mast fed by a half-wavelength piece of low capacitance coaxial cable. The main difference between a normal antenna and the so-called fm antenna is the length. The mast on the fm antenna may also be of rigid construction so the user cannot alter the length and ruin its tuning. Most special antennas offer little or no improvement over the conventional types. Those that do offer better performance do so at the expense of size and cost.

Chapter 16

Troubleshooting FM Stereo

Stereo fm car radios can develop symptoms all their own. Fortunately, the fm multiplex system is simple enough so that it adapts quite well to an easy classification of those symptoms. The major trouble classes revolve around whether or not the system is decoding stereo information as shown by the stereo indicator lamp.

UNLIT STEREO LAMP

When the radio has an unlit stereo indicator lamp, it first should be determined whether or not the stereo signal is being decoded. This can be easily accomplished in one or both of two ways. You can use an fm stereo signal generator of an appropriate type or an *X-Y* oscilloscope. When the generator is used, it is necessary to use either "right only" or "left only" functions. With the generator set to one of these functions and also set to produce 400-Hz modulation, measure the output signal from both channels (Fig. 16-1). Ideally there will be a certain high level output from the active channel and zero output from the passive channel. In reality, however, there will be some spillover. The separation between the two channels in decibels is given by:

$$\text{separation (dB)} = 20 \log \frac{E_{\text{ active channel}}}{E_{\text{ passive channel}}}$$

In most servicing applications, the precise amount of stereo separation is of less concern. The fact that the radio is decoding can be determined subjectively by listening.

The use of the X-Y type oscilloscope is even quicker than using a signal generator. An X-Y oscilloscope, for our purposes, is an oscilloscope with identical gain in both horizontal and vertical channels. In other words, a signal that causes a two-inch deflection when connected to the "V" input will also produce a two-inch deflection when connected to the "H" input. Some shops find this method so useful that they leave an old audio-grade oscilloscope connected across the speaker lines of the stereo workbench. A quick glance at the scope is all that is necessary to determine whether the radio is decoding (Fig. 16-1A). This must, of course, be done while the radio is tuned to a stereo station. An example of the traces that will be found during this type of test is also shown in Fig. 16-2. When the stereo source (whether it is a broadcast or a signal generator) is producing a "right only" signal, only the horizontal input of the scope will receive a signal. The trace, therefore, will lie along the horizontal axis as shown in Fig. 16-2B. A "left only" signal will excite the vertical axis, as in Fig. 16-2C. The only difference between the trace produced by a signal generator and that produced by a broadcaster is that the generator trace will consist of only one line, while the broadcaster's trace will consist of many rapidly changing lines.

Most monaural and undecoded stereo signals will produce a trace that lies on a 45° angle. This is the standard oscilloscope trace produced by applying in-phase signals to both inputs. A phase shift in either channel will change the 45° straight line to an ellipse or even a circle (if both signals are in a quadrature relative to each other). A stereo signal that is being decoded properly will produce a trace that resembles a mass of very angry snakes all twisted together. When troubleshooting a set with a dark stereo lamp, use the X-Y method to determine whether the radio is decod-

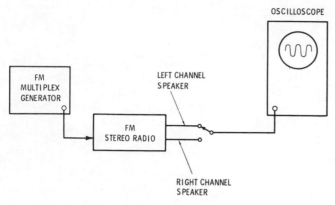

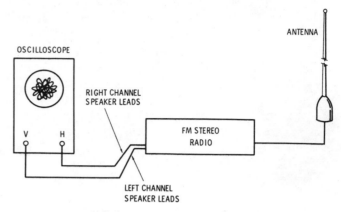

Fig. 16-1. Separation check using a multiplex signal generator and an output level indicator.

(*A*) *Equipment hookup.*

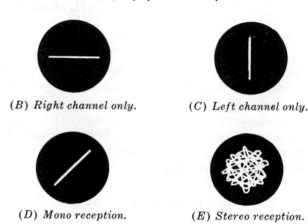

(*B*) *Right channel only.*   (*C*) *Left channel only.*

(*D*) *Mono reception.*   (*E*) *Stereo reception.*

Fig. 16-2. Checking oscilloscope traces.

ing. If it is decoding, you will see a trace such as that shown in Fig. 16-2E. If the set is not decoding, you will see the type of trace illustrated in Fig. 16-2D.

Normal Separation

If the radio is separating the two stereo channels normally yet the indicator lamp is not lit, look for either a defective lamp circuit or a burned out lamp. In most cases, it will prove to be the lamp itself. In a few others, however, the problem could be due to a defective lamp-switching transistor. Try using a resistor to heavily forward-bias the lamp switch. If it still fails to turn on, take it out of the circuit for a closer check on a transistor tester.

In most cases, a dark lamp indicates no separation of the stereo signal. The best method for locating the fault in these cases is by signal tracing (Fig. 16-3). It would be a better test if the radio

were tuned to a stereo generator rather than a broadcast signal during the troubleshooting procedure. This will allow reasonably constant results from one stereo radio to the next. Set the oscilloscope sweep controls so that the horizontal fre-

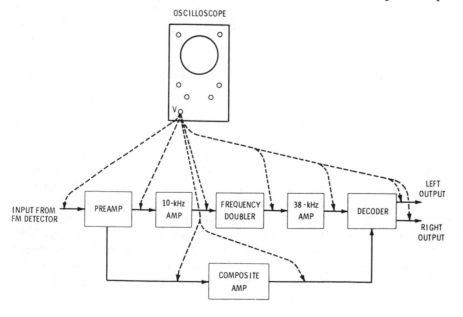

Fig. 16-3. Using an oscilloscope to signal trace an fm stereo radio.

quency is 9500 Hz. This will allow you to view two cycles of the 19,000-Hz pilot and four cycles of the 38,000-Hz regeneration carrier. Trace the signal along the two major paths (composite and carrier regeneration) until the defective stage is located. Once the stage is isolated, it becomes relatively simple to use a vtvm and other instruments to find the specific part that is bad. In most car radios, you will find either a bad transistor or integrated circuit.

No Stereo Separation

One cause of no separation that is frequently overlooked by the inexperienced technician is low radio sensitivity. If the typical fm stereo radio loses one i-f amplifier stage, it may still have sufficient gain to drive the highly sensitive audio amplifiers but not enough to drive the stereo decoder. Most stereo sections have a high operating threshold so that weak and noisy stereo signals will not trigger the system. Some radios even use a threshold detector circuit such as the Bendix circuit shown in Fig. 16-4. The idea of these designs is to prevent the decoder from turning on when there is not enough signal present to offer decent stereo reception. In most such instances, the signal will be capable of rendering acceptable mono reception yet can produce only poor stereo.

In these radios, the sensitivity can be of prime importance. It would be wise to choose a weak station in your area to act as a quick subjective sensitivity check. The criterion is that the station will become all but inaudible if the input trimmer ca-

pacitor is out of alignment. This means that no signal from the *test* station will be heard unless the radio is performing up to par. A quick check for this station is usually sufficient to determine whether or not a particular radio has a sensitivity problem.

If the sensitivity of the radio is low, it will now be necessary to find out what fault has caused this condition. If the defect is something like a bad transistor, simple dc conduction checks will usually suffice. The place to start, in most situations, is the fm i-f amplifier. Connect the common probe of a vtvm to a common dc point. This common point will be *ground* if the i-f amplifier strip uses npn transistors and *i-f B+* if the strip uses pnp transistors. Touch the vtvm probe to the emitter of each i-f transistor in succession. If one of them shows too much, too little, or no dc voltage drop at all, then you may assume that the defect is in that particular stage. In most cases a defect that affects the dc conduction will mean there is a bad transistor or IC in that stage. It is, however, quite possible for all dc voltages to remain normal, yet there will be a defect in that stage causing low gain. Open bypass capacitors and other defects can easily simulate the same symptoms except, of course, the dc conduction changes.

Alignment troubles in older radios are not too common. In newer sets, however, you may find alignment defects fresh from the factory. It may be safely assumed in most cases that an older radio that had an alignment defect would have generated a complaint of poor performance at a much earlier date. In any event, alignment problems are the last possibility to consider in any troubleshooting situation. It is rare, even on a large sampling of new car radios, to find sets with the alignment so far off that radio performance is seriously impaired.

FLICKERING LAMPS

From the customer's point of new, one common symptom is the flickering stereo indicator lamp. This is a very common complaint in automotive fm stereo systems. It must be determined exactly why the lamp is flickering. If the user is attempting to listen to a station beyond the reasonable service zone for that radio and locale, explain to him that this is the cause for the flickering. If, on the other hand, you suspect a defect, then proceed with your attempt to service the radio. Common ailments that can cause the radio to flicker include low sensitivity, a loose connection, and a threshold level that is set too high. It must also be recognized

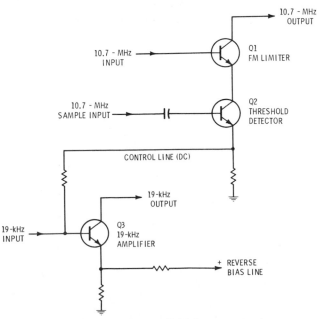

Fig. 16-4. Bendix threshold detector circuit.

that multipath reception, with its resultant signal cancellation zones, can also cause a stereo lamp to flicker.

Some fm stereo radios use an internal balance control that is to be set by the service technician. A large number of the Delco models used in General Motors automobiles use this system. The left to right balance control is usually accessible through a hole in the front panel of the radio. It is a good idea to allow the customer to have the final say on a balance control adjustment. If a hearing impairment in one ear causes him to set the control to an unorthodox balance, it may very well cause him to complain of "one channel dead," if you reset his control to the normal close to center position.

Chapter 17

Miscellaneous Automotive Electronics

There are a large number of accessory devices used with automotive electronic equipment. The first group contains the various types of frequency converters.

FREQUENCY CONVERTERS

Since most frequency converters, except those made for fm broadcast band reception, are of similar design, we will consider them together. In almost every case the converter is used to change some high or very high frequency to a low frequency within the a-m broadcast band. Some of the frequency bands that will be covered by these converters are the shortwave, marine, amateur radio, vhf communication, and fm broadcast bands. Except for those made for the fm broadcast band, all other types are of similar construction.

Shortwave converters are fairly common on cars purchased in Europe. This is because there is considerable broadcast activity on these bands in Europe. In most cases the converter is fixed tuned. In this type of design, the local oscillator in the converter is set to a fixed frequency. The standard a-m band car radio is used as a variable i-f to actually tune in the various stations. Although this may appear to be a shoddy approach to the problem, it need not be. Some of the most expensive professional shortwave communications receivers use the system. If designed properly, the use of a converter ahead of a low-frequency variable i-f offers an improvement in high-frequency stability and image rejection. This assumes, of course, that the converter is crystal controlled. The only real problem is to choose the coverage so that only a small segment of a band is covered at any one setting of the converter. A band of 1-MHz width seems about optimum. It is fortunate that this is the frequency spead of an a-m broadcast band receiver.

Most European converters will have a series of pushbuttons marked L, 49, 41, 31, 25, 19, 13 and so forth. The L marking is the button for the low-frequency *long-wave* broadcast band below 400 kHz. There are a large number of European stations in this band. In the United States, however, it is all but dormant from the normal listener's point of view. The other buttons indicate the approximate wavelength, expressed in meters, of the various shortwave bands. Since these bands do not normally occupy a full 1-MHz slot, the converter is usually aligned so that most of the band will tune toward the center of the a-m dial.

Marine band converters are popular in or near areas where there is much boating activity. A typical marine converter will cover the frequency spectrum between either 2 and 3 MHz or 4 and 5 MHz. The lower band, 2 to 3 MHz, is the more popular of the two bands. The users of these converters like to monitor marine radiocommunications and the weather advisory stations. Many of them are crystal controlled so that the national calling channel, 2182 kHz, is at one specific point on the a-m radio dial. This type of marine converter will become less popular in the future because the lower frequency marine bands are being converted to single sideband (ssb) operation. However, ssb is not practical for car radio conversion. In addition, the FCC is moving most pleasure boat radio traffic to the vhf fm marine band.

Currently available vhf fm communications band converters should work fine on the vhf marine band. Such converters are usually crystal controlled. Since only a small segment of the vhf spectrum (1 MHz) can be received on any one crystal, it will be necessary to specify the frequency of interest. This channel will always appear on the a-m dial at the same point usually close to 800 kHz. Police, fire, business, and marine interests all use the vhf bands. There are two general classifications for vhf converters: high band and low band. The low-band converters usually cover a 1-MHz slice of the radio spectrum between 27 and 54 MHz. They offer reception of the public utility radio services, Citizens band, and the 6-meter amateur band. High band converters cover 1-MHz segments of the 140- to 175-MHz band. This band includes the 2-meter amateur band and police, fire, business, and marine bands. Related converters cover the aviation channels between 110 and 136 MHz. All of these types will feed an output to a special point on the a-m band usually close to 800 kHz. The actual frequency is picked in any given area so that it is between any active broadcast stations.

Do not seem too surprised when you find that these converters are feeding a frequency modulated signal to an a-m receiver. The a-m radio is able to demodulate these signals through a process called slope detection. If the fm signal is tuned such that it is close to one side of the am receiver selectivity skirt, it will encounter a varying frequency response as it deviates through the carrier frequency. This will cause amplitude variations in step with the audio modulation on the signal. These variations can be detected by the diode envelope demodulator used in all a-m car radios. Slope detection may leave much to be desired, but it does offer impressive performance at low cost.

Fig. 17-1 is a block diagram of a converter. It is actually little more than the block of a partial superheterodyne radio. There is an rf amplifier and either a mixer/local oscillator or a converter stage to make the frequency change. Most of the high-quality converters will also include an emitter-follower bandpass amplifier to act as a buffer stage. In most cases the local oscillator will be fixed-tuned to a specific frequency either by a crystal or an LC tank circuit. In some instances, notably on amateur radio converters, the local oscillator will be variable. In these cases, the converter will have its own calibrated dial system. The car radio is used at only one frequency. It acts, in effect, as a fixed-tuned, double-conversion i-f amplifier and detector.

There are also a few converters designed for reception of either the U.S. National Bureau of Stan-

dards time station (WWV) or the Canadian Dominion Observatory time station (CHU). These types are popular with sports car fans who participate in rally events. Possible frequencies for WWV converters are 5, 10, 15, and 25 MHz while CHU converters are usually tuned to 7.335 MHz. Most are set so that the output to the car radio will be either 800 or 1400 kHz. One type, a design published in a popular magazine, offers both 7.335-MHz CHU and 10.000-MHz WWV. It uses one crystal to receive both channels. It seems that a local oscillator set at the midpoint between the two frequencies will give an output for the one closest to 1335 kHz. Then it is only necessary to retune the converter input stage to select which one will be received.

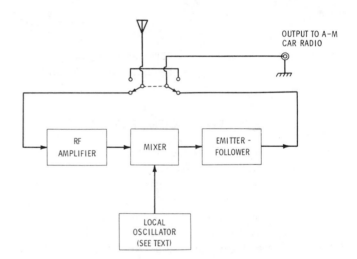

Fig. 17-1. Block diagram of a car radio converter.

Fig. 17-2 is the block diagram of a typical fm broadcast band converter. Since the fm band is approximately 20 MHz wide, the variable i-f converter is next to useless. Also, slope detection is less effective on wideband signals such as in the fm broadcast service. These signals are typically found with ± 75-kHz deviation. An fm car radio converter is actually a complete fm radio including the detectors. The detected audio signal is fed to a solid-state oscillator that operates on a frequency in the a-m band. The audio signal is used to amplitude modulate the oscillator.

The most recent fm converters will have an audio output jack so that an external multiplex adapter can be installed. Many manufacturers offer these adapters complete with the dual audio amplifiers needed for stereo. The frequencies to which the converter changes the fm signal will be one of the two popular converter i-f's (800 or 1400 kHz). In any event, there will be a means of mak-

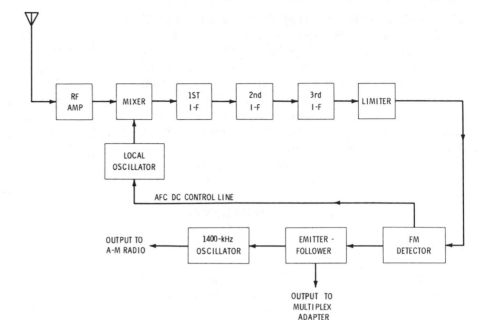

Fig. 17-2. Block diagram of typical fm converter.

ing small adjustments to the modulated oscillator frequency, so that the converter can be operated at a point between any local strong broadcast stations. If the converter output frequency is within 15 kHz of a broadcast station frequency, there will be a possibility of strong heterodyne interference.

POWER CONVERTERS

The power supply used with automotive electronic equipment is of critical importance. The supply must offer the correct voltage level, have adequate reserves of current, and be of the proper polarity for the equipment being operated. Fig. 17-3 shows a circuit that is often used in automotive equipment to allow changes in polarity. Modern American car radios are designed for use in cars where the negative side of the battery is grounded. In fact, this polarity is almost universal. Most foreign cars are also negative ground systems. Only a few foreign brands and certain highway tractor trucks still use the old positive ground system. Fig. 17-3 shows a polarity conversion circuit. If the car has a negative ground system, connect the shorting straps from the power wire (fused) to the positive lead coming from the radio printed-circuit board. Connect another jumper from the radio chassis to the negative lead from the printed-circuit board.

If the radio is to be installed in a positive ground car, it is necessary to connect the chassis to the positive side of the printed-circuit board and the power lead to the negative side of the printed-circuit board. Bypass capacitors will be provided to

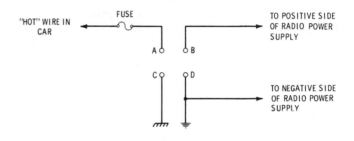

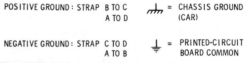

Fig. 17-3. Polarity switching circuit.

allow a low-impedance path to ground for the ac signal currents.

Fig. 17-4 shows a voltage-dropping converter of the type often used in automotive circuits. Bendix made such a circuit (although not this one) in

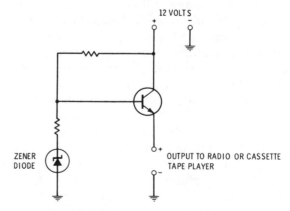

Fig. 17-4. Voltage-dropping converter.

1967. This was the year that Volkswagen switched from 6 to 12 volts in their electrical system. In order to use up existing supplies of 1966 6-volt radios, a voltage dropping converter was needed. In a solid-state radio the line current consumption will vary with the volume level. Because this means wide current excursions, something more than a simple dropping resistor is required. Other dropping converters allow the use of portable radios or cassette machines in a 12-volt automobile. Most of these objects operate from 6, 7.5, or 9 volts dc. The typical converter is designed so that it draws its power through a cigarette lighter socket. In the circuit of Fig. 17-4, the transistor acts as a variable resistor in series with the power lead of the radio. The radio power lead is connected to the emitter of the transistor. The power source from the car battery is connected to the collector of the transistor. A zener diode in the base circuit determines what the output voltage will be. If a heavy current drain drags the radio voltage down, the transistor will tend to turn on a little harder so that the voltage can rise to its higher value. This is the same action found in solid-state voltage regulator circuits.

There are a number of power supplies available for a wide variety of purposes. Most of these use the multivibrator principle of operation. One such circuit is shown in Fig. 17-5. In this configuration, the transistors act as switches to cause a chopped dc to flow through the transformer primary winding. Although the transformer will not respond to a steady dc level, it will treat a chopped dc almost as it would treat ac. The secondary may be either step up or step down as fits the need. In most circuits it is a step-up winding. If the supply is used as a dc-to-ac inverter, there will be no further important secondary circuitry. Most inverters take the 12-V dc primary and convert it to 110 V ac, 60 Hz. If the supply is being used as a dc-to-dc converter, the secondary will feed an appropriate rectifier and filter circuit. Most supplies of this type operate at a high ac frequency. This allows savings in several important areas. One is bulk and weight while the other is cost. Transformers and filter components for 60 Hz are enormous compared with those that will do the same job at 6000 Hz. The zener diodes in Fig. 17-5 are used to protect the switching transistors from high-voltage transients that could easily get into the circuit. In fact, such transients are often generated by this type of circuit. If the problem is particularly bad, the secondary winding may be shunted with a high voltage buffer capacitor.

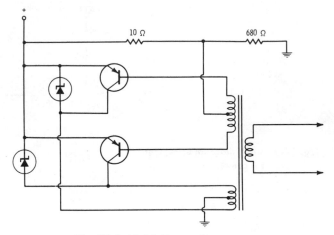

Fig. 17-5. Multivibrator dc converter.

MOBILE PA SYSTEMS

Mobile public address (pa) systems are gaining in popularity. The typical modern mobile pa is a far cry from the older vacuum-tube models. In those designs a 25-watt pa power amplifier and control system could easily occupy the entire front seat of a passenger car. Not only that, they produced a large amount of racket because of the heavy-duty vibrators needed in the power-supply circuit. A modern solid-state pa amplifier in the 25-watt power class may easily be as small as a standard car radio. Also, the modern pa system will offer superior performance and more features than an older design.

The preamplifiers and power amplifiers in a pa unit are similar to those found in car radios. The only real difference is that the pa power amplifier will be in a higher wattage class. The inputs to a mobile pa system are handled a little differently than those on home systems. In the typical home amplifier, the inputs are fed through a switching system. The mobile pa, however, uses a mixer arrangement (Fig. 17-6). To turn an input off, it is necessary to turn down the appropriate volume control. Each control may have a switch that allows the input to be cut off entirely if the need should arise. A mixer must be used at the input because the system may be used where simultaneous programs are desired. One application may be an announcer's voice riding over a musical background.

The speaker system for a mobile pa will usually be of the driver-trumpet (or horn) type. These are better able to withstand the elements of nature than are paper cone types. A rack strapped to the vehicle roof will serve as a mounting support for the speakers. On temporary installations, thin speaker

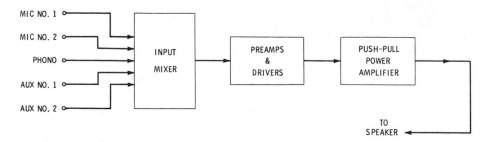

Fig. 17-6. Block diagram of typical mobile pa amplifier.

wire may be routed through the crack at the top of the car window. There is a rubber entrance seal on most cars at this point. The seal will give enough to allow passage of the wire without the danger of pinching. If the installation is to be permanent, bolt the speakers directly to either the roof or the front fender. If the roof is chosen as the sight for the speaker, route the cable underneath the headliner. Connect it to the speaker through a hole cut in the roof directly under the

mount. Make sure the speaker was designed for this application or you may find water leaking in through the hole. Mobile roof speakers include a cork or rubber gasket for sealing the mount base. At the other end of the cable run, try routing the wire from the headliner to the trim molding adorning each side of the windshield. This trim may be hollow to allow passage of headliner courtesy lamp wires. If this routing is followed, it may be possible to do a neat, professional installation.

Index